THE RITUALS NO ONE CAN SEE

Exposure and Response Prevention for Rumination, Mental Reviewing and Silent Reassurance

Helena Mae Prescott

This book provides general educational information about obsessive-compulsive disorder, mental compulsions, and exposure and response prevention. It is not a diagnosis, a substitute for psychotherapy, or individualized medical or mental-health advice. Exposure work can increase distress in the short term. Do not use this book to design exercises that are dangerous, illegal, medically negligent, or inconsistent with ordinary ethical and safety responsibilities. If you have severe symptoms, significant depression, psychosis, substance withdrawal, an unstable medical condition, or uncertainty about whether an exercise is safe, seek qualified professional guidance.
Do not stop prescribed medication or alter medical care because of anything in this book. If you may act on an intention to harm yourself or someone else, or you cannot keep yourself safe, contact local emergency services or a crisis service in your country now. Names and scenarios are composites created for teaching. They are not intended to describe any identifiable person.

ISBN:978-1-911838-66-1

Table of Contents

Preface

Obsessive-compulsive disorder is often explained through visible rituals: washing, checking a lock, arranging objects, or repeating an action. Those examples are useful, but they leave an important treatment problem easy to miss. Compulsions can also occur as mental acts. A person can appear still while spending long stretches reviewing a memory, testing a feeling, neutralizing a thought, silently reassuring themselves, or trying to obtain certainty about what an intrusive thought means.

Exposure and response prevention, usually shortened to ERP, addresses the cycle by bringing a person into contact with a trigger while reducing the compulsive response that follows. When the response is visible, the target can be easier to identify. When the response happens in thought, the difficult question becomes more precise: which mental event is the obsession, and which mental act is the ritual?

This book names that distinction **The Answering Line**. The Answering Line is the point where mental material that has appeared becomes mental work recruited to settle, cancel, prove, review, rehearse, check, or obtain certainty. An intrusive doubt may arrive without permission. The ritual starts when the mind is put to work answering it again and again. The same subject can contain both sides of the line, which is why content by itself is a poor guide.

Many adults with covert OCD already know the basic language of ERP. Some have completed exposures and still found themselves stuck because the mental response continued after the visible exercise ended. Others have been told to stop ruminating without being shown how to identify the specific acts that make rumination compulsive. The result can be a frustrating mismatch: the person is approaching feared material while privately completing the ritual that keeps asking for resolution.

The purpose of this book is to make that hidden response observable enough to work with. It teaches a functional distinction between an obsession and a compulsion, then applies it to rumination, mental reviewing, silent reassurance, feeling checks, neutralizing, recovery checking, and other covert responses. It also shows how exposure can be designed when there is no external object to touch and how response prevention can preserve ordinary thinking, ordinary safety, meaningful relationships, medical care, moral responsibility, and practical problem solving.

The material is written for adults who already suspect or know that OCD is part of the picture, including readers who have tried ERP. Clinicians, support people, and family members may also find the distinctions useful. This is educational material, not a diagnosis or a replacement for individualized treatment. Self-directed exposure is not appropriate for every situation, and no exercise in these pages should override medical advice, emergency care, law, consent, or ordinary safety responsibilities. Readers with severe symptoms, diagnostic uncertainty, significant depression, psychosis, an unstable medical condition, or concerns about safety should work with qualified professionals.

The aim is specific: help you recognize the mental ritual, find the Answering Line, and practice leaving a question unanswered while returning to the life in front of you.

Introduction: When ERP Misses the Ritual

The treatment room can look calm even when a ritual is running at full speed.

Marcus has been working on a health obsession. His assignment is simple on paper: read a short article about an ordinary symptom, notice the uncertainty it brings up, and resist searching for more information. He does that. He closes the browser. He does not call anyone. He does not inspect his body in the mirror. From the outside, the response prevention looks complete.

Inside, a second procedure starts.

He replays the article and checks whether its wording really applies to him. He remembers what a doctor said last year. He compares today's sensation with one from three months ago. He tells himself that serious illness would probably feel different. That sentence brings a small drop in tension, so he repeats the logic with a slightly different set of facts. Ten minutes later he is still doing ERP on the outside and doing reassurance on the inside.

That is the problem this book is built to address.

Obsessive-compulsive disorder can include both repetitive behaviors and repetitive mental acts. Public descriptions of OCD sometimes use visible examples such as washing or checking, but mental acts are part of the condition too. The National Institute of Mental Health lists silent praying or repeating words among examples of compulsions, and describes ERP as a form of CBT that pairs exposure with prevention of the person's usual compulsive response (National Institute of Mental Health [NIMH], 2023). The International OCD Foundation likewise defines exposure broadly enough to include thoughts and images, not only objects or situations, and defines response prevention as choosing not to perform the compulsion after the obsession has been triggered (International OCD Foundation [IOCDF], n.d.-a).

The hard part with a covert ritual is not proving that thoughts can be compulsions. The hard part is deciding which thought is doing which job.

An unwanted image can be an obsession. A deliberate image used to cancel it can be a compulsion. A sentence such as "Maybe I did something wrong" can arrive as an intrusive doubt. The same words can later be repeated deliberately to test whether they still feel frightening. A memory can appear uninvited, then become material for a twenty-minute reconstruction. Content does not classify the act. Function matters.

The distinction has practical consequences. Gillihan and colleagues identified failure to detect mental compulsions as a common problem in ERP for OCD and described mental rituals such as special words, counting, prayer, and repeated internal analysis as targets for response prevention (Gillihan et al., 2012). If a person confronts the trigger while continuing the mental ritual, the exposure plan may be missing the response it was meant to interrupt.

This book gives that boundary a name: **The Answering Line**.

The Answering Line is the point where mental material that has shown up becomes mental work recruited to settle, cancel, prove, check, rehearse, or obtain certainty. You will learn to notice the signal, find the line, and leave the question unanswered long enough to return to the next real action in your day.

That does not mean controlling what appears in your mind. It does not mean forbidding yourself to think. It does not mean calling every reflection, prayer, memory, or act of problem solving a compulsion. A useful response-prevention plan has to preserve ordinary thinking and ordinary safety. The task is narrower:

recognize when a mental act has been hired to do the certainty job OCD keeps reopening.

The informal term “Pure O” is often used for OCD that seems dominated by obsessions, but it can hide the very point this book needs to make. The person may have few visible rituals while doing extensive reviewing, reassurance, neutralizing, checking, or rumination. Mental acts still count as compulsive responses when they serve that function. This book therefore uses **covert OCD** as descriptive shorthand, not as a separate diagnosis.

You will also see an important limit repeated throughout these pages. A self-help book can teach discrimination, planning, and practice. It cannot decide whether every thought is OCD, determine whether a risk is medically acceptable, or replace individualized care. ERP is a well-supported psychological treatment for OCD, and clinical guidance commonly recommends learning it with appropriate professional support, especially when symptoms are severe or the exercise is complex (IOCDF, n.d.-a; NIMH, 2023).

The goal is not a quiet mind. It is a mind that no longer has to finish every internal assignment before you are allowed to continue with your life.

Before you read Chapter 1, take one recent episode and write it as a sequence. What happened first? What appeared in awareness? What did you do with your body? What did you do in your head? Do not edit the list into categories yet. The first skill is seeing the whole loop.

Chapter 1: The Ritual You Missed

Priya's problem starts after an ordinary conversation.

A coworker mentions that a project was delayed because someone failed to pass on a message. Priya cannot remember whether she was copied on an email three weeks earlier. The first thought arrives quickly: *What if it was me?* Her stomach drops. She checks her sent folder once, does not find anything obvious, and goes back to work.

Then she spends the next hour trying to establish what kind of person she is.

Would a responsible person forget a message? If she had seen the email, would she remember seeing it? She reconstructs what she was doing that week. She remembers being tired on Thursday. She tells herself that forgetting one message would not make her dishonest. Then she checks whether that sentence feels like an excuse. The new doubt produces another round of review.

Nothing about the hour would be visible to the people around her. She answers messages, joins a meeting, and looks productive. The ritual is happening in the same place as ordinary planning and memory.

That camouflage matters.

A compulsion can be mental

OCD is commonly described through a cycle of obsessions and compulsions. Obsessions are intrusive, unwanted thoughts, urges, or images. Compulsions can be repetitive behaviors or mental acts performed in response to obsessional distress or a felt rule. NIMH's public guidance includes both visible behaviors and silent repetition among examples of compulsions (NIMH, 2023).

A **mental compulsion** is simply a compulsion carried out primarily in thought.

The label does not depend on whether the thought is logical. It does not depend on whether the sentence is positive or negative. It does not depend on whether another person would call the activity "thinking things through." A mental act becomes important here because of the job it is doing.

Priya is not merely remembering. She is trying to force a verdict about responsibility from an incomplete record. When one answer does not hold, she repeats the process with new evidence.

That is different from an unwanted thought returning.

Imagine that Priya is writing an invoice and the sentence *What if I caused the delay?* pops back into awareness. She did not summon it. She may dislike it. Its arrival is not a ritual. If she then pauses the invoice, searches memory for the email chain, mentally cross-examines herself, and repeats a reassuring sentence until she feels a little safer, those later acts are responses.

The first distinction of this book is therefore small and strict:

What showed up is not the same as what you did next.

You will need that distinction more than any list of common OCD themes.

Relief is a clue, not a definition

Mental compulsions often bring short-lived relief. NIMH notes that people with OCD may not get pleasure from compulsions but can experience temporary relief from anxiety (NIMH, 2023). That makes relief useful evidence that a response may be ritualistic, but it is not a perfect test.

Sometimes a compulsion fails to relieve distress. Priya can review for forty minutes and end more uncertain than she started.

Sometimes an ordinary decision brings relief. Choosing a restaurant can end indecision without becoming OCD.

So ask a more exact question: **What was the mental act supposed to accomplish?**

Was it meant to prove you are safe? Determine whether you are a good person? Establish that a memory is accurate? Make a thought feel less offensive? Confirm that you are attracted enough, guilty enough, certain enough, calm enough, or disgusted enough? Cancel a bad image with a good one? Obtain one final piece of evidence so you can be done?

That intended function tells you more than the emotional result.

Marcus, from the introduction, tells himself that a dangerous illness would probably feel different. The sentence looks like health education. Its function in that moment is silent reassurance. If he were calmly deciding whether to schedule a routine appointment using established medical guidance, the same information could be ordinary problem solving.

Context changes the job.

The invisible families

Mental rituals tend to cluster into recognizable families, even though the words change.

Mental reviewing means replaying or reconstructing past events to determine what happened, what something meant, or whether a feared possibility is true. Grace rereads a meeting in memory to determine whether her joke sounded cruel. Luis reconstructs a drive to make sure he did not hit anything. Elena replays a conversation to decide whether her partner's pause means the relationship is wrong.

Silent reassurance means supplying yourself with evidence or verdicts meant to settle a doubt. Noah reminds himself that he has never acted violently. Keisha recalls the exact words of an earlier diagnostic evaluation. Maya repeats that "thoughts are not actions" until the sentence gives her the right feeling.

Feeling checks turn internal state into evidence. Mei checks whether she feels attraction while looking at a photo. Ben checks whether he feels guilty enough after a moral doubt. Marcus checks whether his body feels "normal."

Neutralizing tries to cancel or correct a mental event. Maya replaces an unwanted image with a pleasant one. Daniel repeats a prayer until it feels sincere enough, even though one ordinary prayer would fit his religious practice. Another person might count, reverse a phrase, imagine a safe ending, or mentally say the opposite of the feared thought.

Rumination, as this book uses the word, is repeated mental problem solving that serves an obsessional question. It is not every period of deep thought and not every recurring thought. The important feature is the repeated attempt to obtain a settlement that never stays settled.

These categories overlap. A review can be reassurance. A feeling check can be rumination. Do not turn the taxonomy into another test you must pass.

You need only enough language to see what the mind is doing.

Why content misleads

OCD can attach significance to many themes: contamination, harm, morality, religion, relationships, health, identity, sex, responsibility, mistakes, memory, symmetry, or other concerns. NIMH notes that obsessions can include aggressive, taboo, contamination, loss, and order-related concerns, among others (NIMH, 2023).

But mental rituals often sound reasonable because they borrow the vocabulary of the theme.

A person with a moral obsession may call review "taking responsibility." A person with relationship fears may call reassurance "being honest with myself." A person with health fears may call checking "being informed." A person with religious fears may call repetition "being sincere." A person with harm fears may call mental reconstruction "making sure everyone is safe."

The values involved can be real. Responsibility matters. Relationships deserve thought. Health deserves appropriate attention. Faith can include prayer. Safety matters.

OCD does not make those domains fake. It recruits them into a process that demands a level of certainty ordinary life cannot provide.

That is why the book will keep returning to function.

The twenty-four-hour observation

For one day, do not try to eliminate mental rituals. Trying to stop them before you can see them clearly often creates a second problem: you start monitoring every thought for evidence that you are "doing OCD."

Instead, collect examples.

When a spike of doubt or discomfort occurs, jot down four brief pieces of information after the fact:

1. The trigger or first mental event.
2. The action you took in the world.
3. The action you took in your mind.
4. What the mental action was trying to get for you.

Keep the fourth line concrete. “To feel better” is often too broad. Try “to know I did not offend her,” “to prove the memory is accurate,” “to feel certain this is attraction,” or “to cancel the image.”

Do not grade yourself for catching a ritual late. If you notice after forty minutes, you have still learned something important: the ritual was not the entire forty minutes of consciousness. There was a point at which you recognized the process.

That point will matter in Chapter 3.

When observation turns into checking

There is one complication. A noticing exercise can become compulsive.

Priya might begin asking every thirty seconds, *Was that thought an obsession or a compulsion? What about that one? Am I ruminating now?* The exercise would then be serving the same certainty demand it was meant to expose.

Use a light touch. Record a few representative examples. If you miss one, let it be missed. If you cannot classify a thought, write “unclear” and continue.

The goal of observation is not perfect accounting. It is to make an invisible behavior visible enough to work with.

The same action can be ordinary or compulsive

The function test becomes clearer when you compare near-identical actions.

Priya reviews a paragraph in a contract because her job requires a final accuracy check. She notices a typo and fixes it. The check had a defined purpose and produced usable information.

Later she rereads an old message that has already been handled. There is no new task. She is listening for a tone that will prove she was not careless. The behavior looks similar, but the job is different.

Marcus pays attention to a new symptom long enough to describe it accurately at an appointment. That is ordinary health behavior.

After the appointment, he scans the same sensation every few minutes to see whether the doctor's reassurance still feels convincing. The scan has become a certainty procedure.

Aisha reads a passage from a religious text because it is part of a study practice. Later she rereads one sentence until she can no longer feel a blasphemous association. The second act is being used to neutralize.

These contrasts matter because a rule such as “never check” or “never review” would be both unrealistic and potentially unsafe. The goal is not to remove normal cognitive functions. It is to stop hiring them for an impossible job.

Why smart people get trapped

Mental rituals often recruit abilities that serve you well elsewhere.

Careful people notice inconsistencies.

Analytical people generate possibilities.

Empathic people imagine how others may feel.

Conscientious people review their work.

Spiritually serious people examine intention.

None of those traits is the enemy.

The problem arises when the ability is placed under a certainty demand that has no natural stopping point.

The better you are at generating explanations, the more explanations you can produce. The better your memory for detail, the more detail you can interrogate. The stronger your concern for others, the more possible harms you can imagine.

This is one reason arguing with the content can be such a poor exit. The mind can always generate another argument.

Response prevention changes the task rather than trying to win it.

A language shift

Listen for words that reveal the hidden job.

"I just need to make sure."

"I should think this through one more time."

"I need to know what that meant."

"I want to check how I feel."

"I should prove that I would never…"

"I need the memory to be clear."

The words are not diagnostic by themselves. Ordinary life includes making sure.

But when the same phrase appears around a repeated, unresolved doubt, it can be a useful warning signal.

Try replacing the question "Is this thought bad?" with "What is my mind asking me to do about it?"

The second question points toward behavior.

That is where ERP has leverage.

One loop from start to finish

Marcus wakes with a mild throat sensation.

Signal: the sensation.

Obsessional question: *What if this is the first sign of something serious?*

His first response is physical. He swallows twice.

Then the covert layer begins.

He compares the sensation with yesterday.

He remembers a sentence from a medical website.

He checks whether the remembered sentence applies to "persistent" symptoms and debates what persistent means.

He tells himself that serious conditions are rare.

He feels better.

Ten minutes later, he notices the sensation again and repeats the argument.

If you look only at the throat, the problem is easy to misread as health concern.

If you look at the sequence, the ritual becomes visible.

There may still be ordinary medical decisions to make. If a symptom meets a clinician's rule for evaluation, Marcus should follow that rule.

ERP does not decide the medicine.

It targets the extra certainty work that begins after ordinary medical behavior has done its job.

Now compare Elena.

Her trigger is her partner being quiet at dinner.

Her mental act is not health comparison. It is emotional comparison.

Did I feel more connected last week? Did he? What did our conversation on Sunday mean?

Different content.

Same loop structure.

Signal.

Question.

Certainty work.

Temporary settlement.

Return of doubt.

That repeated structure is why learning ritual families is more valuable than memorizing theme-specific advice.

Once you can see the loop, you can begin to ask what part belongs to ordinary action and what part belongs to response prevention.

In a Nutshell

Mental compulsions are actions carried out in thought. Their invisibility does not make them less relevant to response prevention. The most useful classifier is function: what the mental act was recruited to settle, prevent, prove, cancel, or make certain.

Relief can point toward a ritual, but it is not the final test. Content can mislead because ordinary values and ordinary thoughts can be recruited into an obsessive-compulsive loop.

For now, notice before you change. Your first useful discovery may be that the ritual does not begin where you thought it did.

Chapter 2: Thought or Ritual

A sentence can change jobs without changing words.

Jonah is lying on the couch when a memory from college appears. He sees the edge of a crowded room and remembers saying something he now finds embarrassing. The thought *Maybe I crossed a line* appears with it.

An hour later Jonah is deliberately repeating the same sentence: *Maybe I crossed a line.* This time he is watching his reaction. If the sentence still produces enough guilt, perhaps that proves he has a conscience. If it feels flat, perhaps that means something worse.

Same words. Different function.

The first appearance may be obsessional material. The later repetition is a feeling check.

If you try to classify mental events by vocabulary alone, covert OCD becomes nearly impossible to read.

Start with origin

The first question is simple: **Did this mental event arrive, or did I recruit it?**

"Arrive" does not mean the thought came from nowhere. A smell, headline, conversation, memory, or bodily sensation can cue it. The point is that you did not intentionally produce it to accomplish a certainty task.

"Recruit" means you deliberately brought something into the mental workspace. You replayed the scene. You asked the question again. You summoned the reassuring fact. You inspected a feeling. You repeated the phrase. You pictured the feared outcome to test your reaction.

This is not a moral distinction. Deliberate does not mean blameworthy. It means the response is a possible target for behavior change.

IOCDF guidance on mental compulsions emphasizes the importance of distinguishing obsessive thinking from compulsive thinking because the latter can then become a target for ERP and non-engagement practice (IOCDF, 2023).

That is the practical value of the distinction.

Then ask about function

Origin alone is not enough. You can deliberately think about something without performing a compulsion.

Maya deliberately remembers what time a train leaves because she needs to buy a ticket. Daniel deliberately reflects on a disagreement because he plans to apologize. Aisha deliberately prays because prayer is part of her faith. Ben deliberately weighs two job offers.

The next question is: **What am I trying to obtain from this mental act?**

Ordinary thinking usually has a workable stopping rule. You gather information, make a decision at the level the situation supports, and move on even though uncertainty remains.

Compulsive thinking asks for a different product. It wants the internal equivalent of a stamped certificate: definitely safe, definitely innocent, definitely attracted, definitely sincere, definitely not dangerous, definitely remembered correctly, definitely diagnosed correctly.

The certificate has an expiration time measured in minutes.

The stop-rule test

Suppose Elena is deciding whether to renew a lease. She compares rent, commute, noise, and space. She cannot predict the future, but she can decide using available facts. When she signs, the decision is done unless genuinely new information appears.

Now suppose Elena is reviewing whether she "really" loves her partner. She checks the warmth she felt at breakfast, compares it with last Tuesday, remembers a moment of irritation, asks whether irritation is evidence, imagines a breakup, checks whether the image creates sadness, then uses the sadness as evidence of love. The process has no external stopping rule.

That difference produces a useful test:

What would allow this thinking to finish?

If the answer is a practical threshold you can actually reach, you may be problem solving.

If the answer is "when I know for sure," "when it feels exactly right," "when there is no remaining doubt," or "when I can no longer imagine a bad interpretation," the process is asking thought to produce something thought cannot reliably supply.

Urges are not actions

Another blur occurs between an urge to ritualize and the ritual itself.

You notice an intrusive doubt and feel a powerful pull to review. The mind presents the first frame of the memory. Did you choose that frame? Maybe not. Then you lean into the sequence, search for the next detail, rewind, compare versions, and interrogate the memory.

The urge and early material can be automatic. Engagement can still become deliberate by degrees.

This matters because “I cannot control what my mind does” is partly true. You cannot guarantee which thought appears. You cannot force uncertainty to vanish. You cannot prevent every memory fragment from arising.

But ERP does not require that control. Response prevention concerns the repeated acts you can begin to identify and decline.

The controllable unit is often much smaller than “stop thinking.”

The gray-zone rule

There will be mental events you cannot classify.

Was that image spontaneous or did you summon it? Did you remember the therapist's sentence automatically or deliberately? Was the first five seconds reflection and the next five reassurance? If you demand certainty about the category, classification itself becomes a ritual.

Use the gray-zone rule: **When classification cannot be settled quickly, do not solve the classification. Ask what action would serve your life either way.**

If you are standing in the grocery aisle debating whether a thought was deliberate, the next useful action may be putting tomatoes in the cart.

If there is a real decision to make, make it at an ordinary standard. If no decision is required, let the thought remain unclassified.

This is not carelessness. It is refusing to build a new obsession around the treatment vocabulary.

Worked distinctions

Consider five pairs.

Pair one: memory. A memory of snapping at your sister appears. That is a mental event. You then replay the conversation six times to establish whether your tone was cruel. That is mental reviewing.

Pair two: reassurance. You recall that a doctor once said your symptom was benign. Memory can arise automatically. You then repeat the doctor's sentence and compare it with today's sensation until anxiety drops. That is silent reassurance.

Pair three: feeling. You notice a flicker of attraction. That feeling is not a ritual. You then scan your body and repeat the stimulus to determine whether the attraction is strong enough. That is a feeling check.

Pair four: prayer. A familiar prayer comes to mind. That is not automatically a compulsion. You then repeat the prayer fourteen times because you cannot tolerate the possibility that the first version was insincere. The repetition may be functioning as neutralizing.

Pair five: planning. You think through the steps of a work task and make a list. That is planning. You then revisit the list every ten minutes to prove you have not forgotten a catastrophic mistake, despite no new information. The repeated checking may be compulsive.

The distinction is not what kind of person you are. It is what the act is doing.

Your first discrimination practice

Take one episode from the observation exercise in Chapter 1. Write it in two columns if you like, but the format is less important than the questions.

For each mental event, ask:

1. Did it show up, or did I deliberately bring it back?

2. If I brought it back, what was I hoping to know, feel, prevent, prove, or settle?
3. Was there a realistic stopping rule?
4. Did I repeat the process after the answer failed to stay answered?
5. What ordinary action was waiting while I kept thinking?

Do not complete this exercise for every thought in the day. Choose one episode.

The skill develops through representative practice, not exhaustive surveillance.

What if the answer is important

This is where covert rituals become persuasive.

But this matters.

Of course it may matter. Whether you harmed someone matters. Health matters. Relationships matter. Moral conduct matters. Work responsibilities matter.

The question is not whether the topic matters. The question is whether repeated internal analysis is producing new usable information.

If there is a concrete action, take it. Check the sent email once if an ordinary workplace question calls for it. Ask a doctor about a persistent symptom according to normal medical guidance. Apologize for a clear mistake. Have the relationship conversation that needs to happen.

Then notice when the task shifts from action to certainty.

OCD frequently demands a second form of responsibility: not only act reasonably, but also prove internally that no bad interpretation remains.

That second demand has no finish line.

The function test under pressure

Classification is easiest when you are calm. The skill has to survive when the content feels urgent.

Maya has an intrusive thought about saying something offensive. Her mind immediately produces a defense: *I would never mean that.*

The defense may be true.

But if Maya's purpose is to learn whether the sentence is factually accurate, she will soon need evidence. She remembers past behavior. She checks emotional reactions. She compares herself with people she considers prejudiced. Each answer creates another exception.

The function test cuts across the content.

"What am I doing right now?"

"Building a case."

"What is the case meant to prove?"

"That the thought does not represent me."

"What would make the proof complete?"

"No remaining doubt."

That last answer exposes the impossible standard.

Four signs that thinking has crossed into ritual

No single sign is decisive, but four patterns are especially useful.

Repetition without new information. You are running the same evidence again.

A moving standard. Every answer creates a new condition that must also be satisfied.

Internal-state dependence. The thinking is not finished until you feel convinced, relieved, guilty, attracted, sincere, or "right."

Life displacement. The question keeps replacing the activity you intended to be doing.

You do not need all four.

One may be enough to pause and ask what function the thinking is serving.

What ordinary reflection looks like

Ordinary reflection can be uncomfortable.

You can think carefully about whether you owe someone an apology and still feel uncertain afterward.

You can consider whether a relationship fits your values and still have mixed feelings.

You can decide to see a doctor and still dislike the uncertainty before the appointment.

The difference is that ordinary reflection accepts a decision threshold lower than certainty.

It says, "I have enough information to choose my next action."

Compulsive analysis says, "I must know the final truth before I am allowed to act."

That distinction protects both sides of the problem. You do not have to stop thinking about important matters. You also do not have to let importance justify infinite analysis.

When the classification changes midstream

A conversation with yourself can begin as useful thinking and become ritual.

Ben spends ten minutes deciding how to respond to his manager's feedback. He chooses two concrete changes.

That part has a job.

Then he starts asking whether the feedback reveals a deeper judgment about his ability. There is no new action. He replays the manager's wording and checks whether it sounded disappointed.

The process crossed the Answering Line during the same sitting.

You are allowed to stop at the point where the job changes.

You do not have to condemn the useful first ten minutes because the next twenty became compulsive.

A difficult category: deliberate exposure thoughts

ERP sometimes asks you to deliberately bring up a feared thought.

That means “deliberate” cannot automatically mean “compulsion.”

Suppose Maya reads the sentence “Maybe I offended someone” as a planned exposure.

She deliberately produces the thought, but the function is not to obtain certainty.

She is contacting the feared cue and preventing the usual reassurance.

Now suppose she repeats the sentence to see whether she still feels guilty.

The same deliberate thought has become a feeling check.

This is why the classification requires both origin and function.

A planned exposure is recruited to contact uncertainty.

A mental compulsion is recruited to escape, settle, cancel, or verify uncertainty.

The wording can be identical.

Another gray category is compassionate self-talk.

If Maya tells herself, “I can survive feeling upset,” and then continues her day, the statement may be a flexible coping response.

If she repeats it until she can prove she will definitely cope with every future outcome, it may have become reassurance.

Do not classify techniques once for all time.

Ask what they are doing in the moment.

That question keeps treatment flexible without making every thought suspicious.

Principles to Remember

A thought is not classified by its wording. Ask whether it arrived or was recruited, then ask what the recruited thinking was meant to accomplish.

Ordinary thinking can tolerate a stopping rule based on available information. Compulsive thinking tends to keep reopening the question because it is trying to obtain complete certainty or a perfectly convincing feeling.

Gray areas do not have to be solved. If classification itself becomes a checking project, leave the category uncertain and return to the next useful action.

Chapter 3: Find the Answering Line

The easiest place to imagine the Answering Line is not in OCD.

Suppose you are reading a novel and suddenly wonder whether you locked the back door. The thought appears. You remember locking it. You continue reading.

Now change one detail. You remember locking it, but the memory does not feel vivid enough. You rebuild the scene: your hand on the lock, the click, the keys in your pocket. You compare the image with yesterday's image. You test whether you can picture the door open. You notice that you can, and the ability to picture it becomes evidence that perhaps it happened.

The original question took one second.

The answer became a project.

The **Answering Line** is the point where you cross from receiving mental material into recruiting mental work to settle it.

It is not a neurological border. It is a practical teaching device. You will not see it on a scan. You use it because it gives you a place to intervene.

Signal, urge, response

Break a covert ritual into three pieces.

Signal: An intrusive thought, image, urge, memory fragment, sensation, or doubt appears.

Urge: You feel pressure to do something with it. Review. Check. Explain. Cancel. Reassure. Test.

Response: You begin the mental act.

These pieces can occur in less than a second. With repetition, they can feel fused.

Daniel notices the thought *What if I missed someone in the crosswalk?* while driving. Immediately he feels a pull to replay the last intersection. A frame appears automatically. Then he starts scanning the frame for shapes, colors, and movement.

The line is not between "thinking" and "not thinking." It is between the material and the recruited search.

Why late catching counts

People often turn this skill into perfectionism.

"If I only notice after twenty minutes, I failed."

No. You noticed.

At first, the Answering Line is easier to see in retrospect. You come out of a review and identify the point where the question changed from appearing to being worked. Later you may notice after five minutes. Later still, after thirty seconds.

The learning process runs backward before it runs forward.

The same is true of many habits. You first recognize them after completion, then during the act, then closer to the cue. The important measure is not instant detection. It is whether detection gives you another opportunity to choose.

The micro-ritual problem

Not all mental compulsions last an hour.

Aisha sees a distressing word and silently says a short phrase to make it feel neutral. The whole response takes one second. Because the ritual is so small, she assumes it cannot matter.

Frequency can make a small act significant. If the phrase is repeated hundreds of times, it can become a constant condition for moving through the day.

The Answering Line helps with micro-rituals because it asks a tight question: **What did you add after the signal?**

Sometimes the added act is a single word.

Sometimes it is a glance inward to check a feeling.

Sometimes it is a tiny mental “No, that's not true.”

The size of the act does not determine its function.

Do not hunt the line

There is a paradox here. If you stare at your mental stream trying to catch the precise millisecond of choice, you can create another form of monitoring.

The line is not a laboratory measurement. It is enough to identify a usable region.

Think in rough sequence:

“Trigger. Doubt. Pull to review. Then I was reconstructing.”

That is enough.

You do not need to decide whether the first image in the reconstruction was voluntary. You need to notice that active reconstruction is happening now.

Three ways the line hides

The first hiding place is **speed**. The ritual starts so quickly that it looks simultaneous with the obsession.

The second is **good intention**. The response sounds responsible, kind, spiritual, informed, or rational.

The third is **habit**. You have performed the response so many times that it arrives as a procedural reflex.

None of those makes the response immutable.

Habit reduces the feeling of choice. Practice can widen the gap enough to make a different action possible.

The after-the-fact map

Use one episode today and map it after it ends. Do not monitor in real time.

Write:

"Signal: ______."

"Urge: ______."

"Response I added: ______."

"What I wanted the response to give me: ______."

"Ordinary action I could return to: ______."

If you cannot identify the response, leave the line blank. Try another episode later.

If you can identify it, do not immediately redesign your whole treatment. Chapter 9 will give you a more complete non-engagement method. For now, the aim is discrimination.

A difficult example

Ben receives a performance review at work. His manager gives him four positive comments and one suggestion: send shorter emails.

On the train home, the sentence *She thinks I'm incompetent* appears.

Ben argues back: *If she thought that, she would not have praised the project.*

Was that response reassurance? Probably.

Then another thought appears: *But maybe the praise was just politeness.*

Ben notices the loop and says, *Maybe she does think I'm incompetent.*

Is that response prevention? It could be.

Then he repeats *maybe she does* twenty times, checking whether he feels sufficiently accepting of uncertainty.

Now the treatment phrase has become a feeling check.

This example matters because no sentence is protected from ritualization. Even a good ERP phrase can cross the Answering Line if you recruit it to manufacture a state.

The function stays in charge.

The line is easier to see in behavior than in feeling

Some readers wait for an internal signal that says, *Now I am choosing.*

That signal may never arrive.

Habitual mental rituals can feel involuntary even after you have started participating in them. The useful test is not whether choice feels vivid. It is whether there is a next act you can decline.

Daniel is already replaying the intersection before he notices.

He cannot undo the first ten seconds.

He can decline the next rewind.

He can stop searching for a pedestrian-shaped image.

He can return attention to driving.

That is enough for one repetition of response prevention.

Catching the ritual in layers

Think of detection in four layers.

Afterward: "I spent half an hour reviewing."

During: "I have been reviewing for five minutes."

Near the start: "I just began reconstructing."

At the urge: "I want to reconstruct, and I have not started."

These are not levels you must graduate through in order.

You may catch one ritual at the urge and another only afterward.

The goal is simply to create more opportunities at earlier points over time.

The danger of retrospective perfection

After learning the Answering Line, people sometimes review old episodes to identify exactly where every ritual began.

That can become another mental compulsion.

You do not need to audit your entire history.

Use recent, representative examples.

If one episode is unclear, leave it unclear.

The method is meant to support present behavior, not produce a perfect archive of past cognition.

A two-minute live experiment

Choose a harmless recurring thought, not your most distressing obsession.

When it appears, notice the pull to do something with it.

If you catch a mental response beginning, stop the response without trying to remove the thought.

Then complete one simple action in the environment: put away a dish, answer a neutral message, continue reading, or return to the task on your screen.

Two minutes later, do not evaluate the quality of your non-engagement.

The experiment ends with the action.

That ending is deliberate. It teaches the nervous system and your attention that the day can continue without an internal closing ceremony.

The Answering Line during a conversation

The line does not only appear when you are alone.

Keisha is talking with a friend when a moral doubt appears about something she said.

She hears the friend continue speaking, but internally she starts reviewing her own last sentence.

The review is so fast that she misses the next part of the conversation.

Then she notices.

She has a choice.

She could ask her friend to repeat the last sentence, not for reassurance, but because she genuinely did not hear it.

She could also keep reviewing and pretend to listen.

The response-prevention action is ordinary and slightly awkward: "Sorry, I missed that last part. Can you say it again?"

This example shows why returning to life may require repair.

Non-engagement is not a demand to perform perfectly while distracted by intrusive material.

It lets you make a normal correction and then continue.

The Answering Line is not there to make you hyper-aware of your mind.

It is there to help you notice when internal work starts replacing the external life you are trying to participate in.

In a Nutshell

The Answering Line separates what appears from the mental work you recruit to answer it. Use three rough pieces: signal, urge, response.

You do not need to catch the line instantly or locate it with perfect precision. Late recognition is useful. Tiny rituals still count. Helpful phrases can become rituals if their job changes.

The skill is not constant self-monitoring. It is learning to recognize, often after the fact at first, where the internal assignment began.

Chapter 4: Rumination Is Mental Work

Rumination is a dangerous word because it can mean too many things.

People use it for any repetitive thought, any period of worry, any memory that will not leave, or any difficult reflection. This book uses it more narrowly. **Rumination** is repeated mental problem solving that becomes compulsive when its function is to settle an obsessional doubt or obtain relief or certainty.

That definition protects two truths at once.

Thoughts can recur without your permission.

You can also choose to keep working on a recurring question.

Sofia sees both happen on the same evening.

She is washing a pan when the thought *What if I don't love him enough?* appears. She did not decide to have it. Ten minutes later she is sitting at the table reviewing the last six months of her relationship, comparing desire levels, recalling vacations, and testing how she feels while imagining a breakup.

The first sentence arrived.

The case conference that followed was mental work.

Recurrence is not rumination

An intrusive thought can return many times even when you refuse to analyze it.

That distinction matters because a reader may try response prevention and conclude it has failed: "I stopped ruminating, but the thought came back."

The return of the thought does not prove that you ruminated. Response prevention does not control recurrence.

Exposure-based treatment asks for contact with the trigger and prevention of the compulsive response, not guaranteed removal of unwanted thoughts. Current professional descriptions of ERP emphasize confronting obsessional cues and resisting ritual behavior rather than waiting for thoughts to disappear (IOCDF, n.d.-a; NIMH, 2023).

If the thought returns twenty times and you begin twenty fewer investigations, something important has changed even if the thought count is unchanged.

The problem-solving disguise

Rumination often feels productive because it uses genuine cognitive tools.

You remember.

You compare.

You infer.

You test explanations.

Those are useful operations when a problem has enough information to support a decision. The trouble begins when the question requires impossible certainty or the operations keep repeating after they have stopped producing new information.

Ask the **decision test**:

What real-world decision will this thinking allow me to make?

Sofia may need to decide whether to have a conversation with her partner. That is a real decision.

She does not need to determine the exact percentage of love she feels, establish what every past moment "really meant," or prove that no future doubt will appear. Those are verdict tasks with no stable measurement.

Ben may need to revise how he writes emails. He does not need to determine whether his manager secretly thinks he is incompetent.

Priya may need to check a specific work record once. She does not need to reconstruct her moral character from the feeling tone of a memory.

The one-question rule

When rumination begins, identify the practical question hidden underneath it.

Examples:

"Do I need to send an apology?"

"Do I need to book a routine medical appointment?"

"Is there a decision about this relationship I am prepared to make today?"

"Is there a work action due now?"

Then answer only at an ordinary standard with information already available or information that can reasonably be obtained.

If no action is required, the rest of the thinking may be an attempt to obtain internal certainty rather than solve a practical problem.

The one-question rule is not "never think." It is "give thinking a job that can actually finish."

Why postponement can help and fail

Some people find it useful to delay rumination: "I am not solving this at 9:15. If it still needs attention, I will look at it at 6:00."

The technique can create distance from the immediate urge. But it can also become a contract with OCD: *I promise I will give you a full hearing later.*

If 6:00 becomes a scheduled ritual hour, the method has not served its purpose.

Use postponement only when it supports disengagement. When the scheduled time arrives, ask the decision test again. If there is no practical action, you do not owe the question a trial simply because it waited.

When the mind says this is different

Rumination survives by exception.

This one is different because the stakes are high.

This one is different because I almost remember.

This one is different because I have new evidence.

Sometimes there really is new evidence. A lab result arrives. A person tells you what happened. Your manager sends a new instruction. Ordinary life changes the facts.

The useful question is not "Could this be different?" Almost anything could.

Ask, "Is there genuinely new external information that changes the decision I need to make?"

If yes, respond to it.

If no, notice the attempt to reopen the internal trial.

A practice with a stopping rule

Choose one low-to-moderate rumination loop. Do not start with your most frightening topic.

Write the practical decision, if any, in one sentence.

Set an ordinary stopping rule before you think. For example: "I will read the email once and decide whether a reply is required." Or: "I will write down the facts I already know and decide whether I need to ask my doctor at my next scheduled appointment."

Complete the action.

Then stop the certainty work even if the emotional sense of completion does not arrive.

That final part is response prevention.

Rumination versus worry

Rumination and worry can overlap in everyday language. Clinically, different traditions use the terms in different ways.

For this book, the distinction is functional rather than diagnostic.

Worry often leans toward future possibilities.

Mental review often leans toward the past.

Rumination can move in either direction when the person repeatedly tries to solve an obsessional question.

You do not need to win a vocabulary debate before using response prevention.

Ask whether the mental work is producing a decision or merely another round.

The false promise of insight

Rumination sometimes offers a sophisticated bargain:

"If you understand why this thought bothers you, you will be able to stop having it."

That promise can keep people searching for the perfect origin story.

Maybe the thought came from childhood.

Maybe it reflects a personality trait.

Maybe it means a hidden value conflict.

Maybe it appeared because you were tired.

Some self-understanding can be useful. Therapy may involve careful formulation.

But insight is not a guaranteed off-switch for obsessions.

If the search for "why" is repeated each time distress appears, the search itself may become a ritual.

Ask what you would do differently if you found the explanation.

If there is no action beyond feeling certain, the investigation may not need another hour.

The "one more angle" problem

Rumination rarely repeats in exactly the same words.

It changes angle.

You decide the feared interpretation is unlikely.

Then the mind asks whether "unlikely" is good enough.

You decide it is.

Then the mind asks whether your confidence is based on denial.

You answer.

Then it asks why you were so quick to answer.

Because the surface question changes, the loop can feel productive.

Track the function instead.

Every angle is still trying to obtain the same settlement.

This is one reason the Answering Line is more useful than a list of sentences to avoid.

A decision window

For a genuine problem that deserves thought, create a decision window.

Write the exact decision.

Choose the information you will use.

Set the time limit.

Make the best available choice.

Then close the window.

If the question returns later without new information, treat the return as a cue for non-engagement.

This method is not about making fast decisions.

A serious decision can have a long window.

The important part is that the window is attached to a real choice, not to the arrival of a perfect feeling.

Rumination after genuine conflict

A real conflict can trigger both useful reflection and OCD.

Sofia argues with her partner.

Later, she thinks about what happened.

She identifies one thing she said unfairly and decides to apologize.

Useful reflection.

Then she asks why she said it.

She generates three explanations.

She asks which explanation reveals her "true" feelings.

She remembers another argument from two years ago.

She compares the two.

She checks whether she feels enough remorse.

The task has shifted.

The apology can happen without a complete theory of her relationship or character.

This is an important principle: **a real event does not make every thought about it useful.**

OCD can attach to genuine mistakes, illness, grief, conflict, or uncertainty.

ERP is not reserved for obviously irrational content.

The behavioral question remains: what action is actually required, and what extra mental work is trying to produce certainty beyond that action?

When the real-world task is complete, the rest can remain unresolved.

Principles to Remember

Rumination is not the same as a thought recurring. In this book, it means repeated mental problem solving recruited to settle an obsessional doubt.

Useful thinking has a workable job and a stopping rule. Compulsive thinking keeps reopening the question because it wants certainty or the right feeling.

A practical decision can be handled at an ordinary standard. The remaining internal trial does not have to be completed.

Chapter 5: Mental Review Keeps Asking

Grace leaves a meeting with no clear problem to solve.

The project was approved. Nobody objected to her proposal. Her manager thanked the group and moved to the next item.

On the walk back to her desk, Grace remembers a joke she made near the end. She sees one coworker's face in memory and cannot tell whether the expression was amusement or discomfort.

The memory arrives.

Then she begins improving the evidence.

She replays the sentence with different tones. She estimates how long the coworker paused before smiling. She reconstructs who was looking at whom. She remembers a similar joke from last month and compares the reactions. When she reaches a version that seems harmless, she feels relief for about thirty seconds.

Then she wonders whether relief itself means she is minimizing what she did.

The review restarts.

Memory is not a recording

Mental reviewing becomes compelling because it promises access to a record that feels as if it should be recoverable. If you could replay the event clearly enough, perhaps you could know what happened and what it meant.

Human memory does not function like a video file that can be repeatedly opened without interpretation. Memory research in OCD gives us a narrower and more useful point: repeated checking is not a dependable route to greater confidence. Studies have found that people can become less confident in what they remember after repeated checking even when objective accuracy does not decline in the same way (Tolin et al., 2001; van den Hout & Kindt, 2003).

That matters in OCD because the review is often asking memory to do more than ordinary memory can do.

Luis does not merely remember driving home. He tries to prove that there was no moment in which he could have hit a pedestrian without noticing. Grace does not merely remember a joke. She tries to establish what every person inferred from it. Jonah does not merely recall a party. He tries to reconstruct his intent from years ago.

The mental archive is being asked to produce a verdict.

Four forms of review

Mental review often takes one of four forms.

The first is **sequence reconstruction**. You rebuild the order of events: where you stood, what you touched, which road you took, what happened before and after.

The second is **meaning reconstruction**. You replay words, facial expressions, or sensations to determine what they "really" meant.

The third is **intent reconstruction**. You inspect what you remember thinking or feeling in order to decide what kind of motive you had.

The fourth is **counterfactual review**. You imagine what you would have done under slightly different conditions and use the imagined result as evidence about the past.

All four can be ordinary in moderation. Police interviews, medical histories, apologies, and work investigations sometimes require careful reconstruction.

The ritual version is distinguished by repetition, function, and the certainty standard it is trying to meet.

The new-evidence test

Before reviewing, ask one question:

Is there new external information that makes a practical review necessary?

Grace receives no complaint, no message, and no new fact. Her review is powered by a remembered expression and an urge to know.

Luis hears no impact, sees no accident, and receives no new report. His urge is to replay the drive until memory feels complete.

Now imagine Luis receives a legitimate notice from his employer that a company vehicle was involved in an incident at a specific time. That is new external information. Appropriate review and reporting may be required.

ERP is not a rule against remembering. It is a way of declining repeated certainty work when no practical task calls for it.

Review after exposure

One of the most important hidden rituals happens after an exposure.

You complete the exercise. During it, you resist the main compulsion. Then, ten minutes later, you begin grading what happened.

Did I really allow uncertainty?

Was I secretly reassuring myself?

Did my anxiety drop too much?

Did I choose the right statement?

Was that genuine acceptance or was I forcing it?

You can spend more time reviewing the exposure than doing it.

This matters because response prevention is not over when the formal exercise ends. If the exposure is followed by a certainty audit, the mind has found a delayed route back to the same job.

A useful exposure plan therefore names the **post-exposure review** in advance.

You might write: “For the next hour I will not replay the exercise to decide whether I did it correctly. I will record only whether I performed the named ritual.”

That gives tracking a behavioral target instead of an internal performance score.

The memory-confidence trap

When people repeatedly check a memory, they often expect confidence to rise. The subjective result can be the opposite: the more the memory is examined, the less trustworthy it feels.

Research on repeated checking has found that repeated checking can reduce memory confidence while accuracy remains comparatively intact, a pattern demonstrated in OCD and experimental checking work (Tolin et al., 2001; van den Hout & Kindt, 2003).

The practical lesson is modest.

Do not use the loss of confidence caused by repeated review as proof that more review is needed.

If the tenth replay feels blurrier than the first, that is not a command to produce an eleventh.

Leave one memory unreconstructed

Choose a low-stakes episode that you have been replaying.

Write one sentence naming the question: "Did she think I was rude?" or "Did I notice that bump while driving?"

Then write the ordinary action, if any. Perhaps there is none. Perhaps there is a clear apology to make. Perhaps there is a standard reporting process.

After that, leave the memory unreconstructed for a defined period, such as thirty minutes.

When the urge to replay appears, use a brief non-engagement response: "I am not rebuilding this right now." Do not add a reassuring reason.

Return to an activity that was already part of your day.

The goal is not to feel confident about the memory. It is to stop requiring memory confidence before you continue.

If a real mistake is possible

OCD treatment does not remove ordinary accountability.

If you learn that you did make a mistake, deal with the mistake. Correct the invoice. Apologize. Follow the safety procedure. Seek medical care when a real medical issue calls for it.

Response prevention applies to the extra trial that asks for perfect proof about what the mistake means, whether every consequence has been prevented, whether your motive was pure, or whether the memory is now certain enough.

Ordinary responsibility ends somewhere.

The ritual tries to erase that boundary.

Why checking can make confidence worse

Luis believes one more replay will settle the drive.

He reconstructs the intersection and feels ninety percent certain that nothing happened.

Then he checks again.

The second replay contains a gap.

Now he is seventy percent certain.

The change in confidence feels like new evidence, but the only new event was another act of checking.

Experimental studies of repeated checking have found a pattern in which repeated checking can reduce subjective memory confidence while objective accuracy remains comparatively intact (van den Hout & Kindt, 2003). That finding does not mean every act of remembering damages memory. It does explain why confidence is a poor stopping rule for compulsive review.

If confidence is the target, reviewing can create the very uncertainty that calls for more review.

Memory gaps are ordinary

A complete memory of an ordinary day would be extraordinary.

You do not remember every pedestrian you passed, every word in a meeting, or every movement while cooking.

OCD can turn normal gaps into suspicious absences.

"If I cannot remember it, perhaps something happened."

Then the mind treats lack of evidence as a reason to investigate.

A more ordinary standard asks whether there is external evidence of a problem or a practical reason to respond.

If not, the gap can remain a gap.

You do not need to fill it with a reconstructed story.

Mental review and responsibility

Review often feels morally required.

Grace thinks that if she stops replaying the joke, she is refusing accountability.

Luis thinks that if he stops reconstructing the drive, he is being careless about public safety.

Responsibility, however, has procedures.

If there is a concrete reason to believe harm occurred, follow the appropriate procedure.

If there is a clear mistake, repair it.

If there is no new information and the review is trying to reach impossible certainty, continuing the review does not create more responsibility.

It creates more review.

The hard practice is allowing the possibility that you might someday learn something you would need to address, without performing a private investigation every time the possibility can be imagined.

A post-event boundary

Choose one event you routinely review.

Before it happens, decide what ordinary debriefing is allowed.

For a work meeting, perhaps you will write down action items once.

For a social event, perhaps you will respond only to concrete feedback.

For driving, perhaps you will follow the same normal safety and reporting rules used by other responsible drivers.

Then add one sentence:

"After the ordinary debrief, I will not reconstruct the event to improve certainty."

The boundary is useful because it is set before the emotional demand arrives.

Review disguised as empathy

Grace worries that stopping review will make her less considerate.

She uses replay to imagine every way a coworker could have received her words.

That looks empathic.

The problem is that empathy has no stopping rule when it is asked to eliminate all risk of misunderstanding.

Ordinary empathy might say, "That comment could have landed badly. If I notice discomfort or receive feedback, I can address it."

Compulsive empathy says, "I must simulate every private reaction until I know nobody was hurt."

The second task is impossible because other minds are not fully accessible.

You can care about impact and still accept incomplete information.

The same distinction applies to parents, partners, managers, and friends.

Responsiveness is based on what you can reasonably know.

Mental review tries to make you responsible for what you cannot know.

Response prevention returns responsibility to its ordinary boundaries.

In a Nutshell

Mental review takes memory and turns it into an investigative tool. The problem is not remembering. The problem is asking repeated reconstruction to deliver a level of certainty the record cannot provide.

Look for sequence, meaning, intent, and counterfactual review. Ask whether new external information creates a real task. Plan for post-exposure review before it starts.

When a memory feels less trustworthy after repeated checking, do not treat the loss of confidence as a request for another round.

Chapter 6: Reassurance Without Another Person

Noah knows he should stop asking his partner whether he is dangerous.

He has read about reassurance seeking. He has noticed the pattern: an intrusive harm image appears, he asks a question, his partner tells him he is safe, and relief lasts until the next image.

So Noah stops asking.

Then he starts answering himself.

I have never hurt anyone.

I was upset by the thought, so I clearly do not want it.

My therapist said intrusive thoughts can be ego-dystonic.

People who really wanted this would not worry about it this much.

The conversation has moved inside.

The certainty job is unchanged.

Reassurance is a function

Research on reassurance seeking in OCD has examined why people repeatedly ask for confirmation and how reassurance relates to checking. Parrish and Radomsky found important similarities between reassurance seeking and checking, including attempts to reduce uncertainty or distress (Parrish & Radomsky, 2010). Later work developed and validated a measure that distinguishes overt and covert forms of reassurance seeking, including in a sample of people diagnosed with OCD (Radomsky et al., 2021).

For this book, **silent reassurance** means internally supplying evidence, arguments, remembered statements, or verdicts intended to make an obsessional doubt feel settled.

It can sound intelligent.

It can even be factually true.

The issue is not whether the reassuring sentence is false. It is whether you are repeating it because the obsession demands another guarantee.

The therapist-quote ritual

Keisha has a sentence from a previous evaluation: "These symptoms fit OCD."

At first, the sentence helps her understand a diagnosis.

Later, whenever she has a disturbing thought, she repeats the sentence until she feels convinced again.

Then a new doubt appears: *What if I described my symptoms incorrectly during the evaluation?*

Keisha searches memory for how the appointment went. She recalls examples she gave. She reconstructs the clinician's tone. She visits an online symptom checklist.

The helpful sentence has become an entry point to a reassurance chain.

This does not mean psychoeducation is harmful. Accurate information matters.

It means information can be used in two different ways: once to learn, or repeatedly to neutralize uncertainty.

The Answering Line in reassurance

Use the Chapter 2 question: **What am I trying to get from this?**

If you are reading about OCD because you need to understand a treatment method, that has a practical endpoint.

If you are rereading the same paragraph for the eighth time to prove that your exact thought pattern still qualifies, the function has changed.

If you remember your doctor's advice because you need to follow a treatment plan, that is ordinary use of information.

If you repeat the doctor's words whenever uncertainty spikes because you need immediate certainty that nothing serious is wrong, the words may be serving reassurance.

The sentence is not the ritual by itself.

The job is.

External and internal reassurance can trade places

A person who stops asking others may temporarily increase silent reassurance.

Another person may do the reverse. They stop arguing with themselves but begin asking a spouse, friend, forum, search engine, chatbot, or clinician.

The format changes. The function does not.

That is why a response-prevention plan should name both routes.

For example:

“My target is not only asking my partner whether I offended her. It is also replaying her tone, reminding myself that she smiled, searching messages for evidence, and telling myself she would speak up if she were angry.”

The target becomes specific enough to catch substitutions.

Reassurance versus information

You do not need to stop asking questions.

Medical care requires information. Work requires clarification. Relationships require communication. Learning ERP requires instruction.

A useful distinction is whether the answer changes an action.

Suppose Marcus has a new symptom that meets his doctor's stated rule for calling the office. He calls. The answer changes what he does. That is appropriate information seeking.

Now suppose the doctor has already said no further check is needed unless a listed change occurs. Marcus asks the same question again because his confidence in the answer has fallen. The second request may be reassurance.

The boundary cannot be reduced to "one question is safe, two are OCD." Context matters.

Use ordinary standards and, when medical or safety questions are genuinely unclear, ask a qualified professional rather than making ERP rules from a book.

A neutral refusal to decide

Silent reassurance often needs a response that does not secretly answer the question.

The following are examples, not magic phrases:

"I am not settling that now."

"That question can stay open."

"I have the urge to prove it, and I am not doing the proof."

"I can act on what is actually required without finishing this argument."

A phrase becomes unhelpful if you repeat it until you feel safe. Say it once, if needed, then return to the activity.

Sometimes no phrase is better. You notice the urge and keep making dinner.

The response is behavioral: you decline the reassurance procedure.

When support people are involved

A partner or friend does not have to become cold.

They can acknowledge distress without providing repeated certainty.

Instead of "I promise you did nothing wrong," a support person might say, "I can see this is pulling you toward the same question. What does your response-prevention plan say?"

That answer may still become ritualized if it is delivered on demand fifty times. The relationship needs boundaries that are agreed outside the spike.

If you are working with a clinician, involve them in planning how reassurance reduction will work. Sudden, punitive refusal can damage trust and is not the point.

The one-answer experiment

Choose one recurring reassurance question.

Write the ordinary information you already have. Do this once, not repeatedly.

Then choose a period in which you will not seek another internal or external verdict unless genuinely new information changes the practical decision.

Notice the routes your mind proposes.

It may offer a memory.

A statistic.

A diagnostic label.

A feeling.

A comparison with another person.

A line from this book.

Each route is asking to cross the Answering Line.

You do not have to follow it.

Reassurance has a half-life

The relief from reassurance often fades quickly.

That fading is not a defect in the person giving the answer.

It is built into the type of question being asked.

If the obsession asks for complete certainty, no ordinary answer can satisfy it permanently. A spouse can say, "You did not offend me." The mind can ask whether the spouse is hiding irritation. A doctor can say, "This does not require another test." The mind can ask whether the doctor understood every detail.

Reassurance is therefore vulnerable to an infinite appeal process.

The answer may be perfectly reasonable.

The court never closes.

Certainty borrowed from authority

Authority can make reassurance especially compelling.

A clinician's sentence.

A religious leader's interpretation.

A legal opinion.

A trusted friend's judgment.

A book's explanation.

The authority may be genuine, but repeated use can still become ritualistic.

There is a difference between following professional advice and mentally repeating the advice every time doubt spikes.

One is behavior based on guidance.

The other is guidance converted into a reassurance token.

This book should not become one of those tokens. If you notice yourself rereading a paragraph to prove your exact fear is harmless, close the book and return to your treatment plan or ordinary task.

Covert reassurance through comparison

Comparison is another silent route.

You compare your thought with a story about someone who actually acted badly.

You compare your relationship feeling with a friend's.

You compare your memory with how "a guilty person" would remember.

You compare your symptom with a picture online.

The comparison seems like evidence gathering.

Its function may be to place you on the safe side of a line.

When you notice the same comparison repeated, ask whether the categories are serving a real decision or merely a verdict.

Reassurance reduction is gradual for some people

A reader may be seeking reassurance dozens or hundreds of times per day.

Stopping every route at once can be impractical.

Work with a clinician if symptoms are severe.

A graded approach can target one recurring question or one context first. The aim is not to preserve reassurance forever. It is to create practice opportunities that are specific enough to complete.

For example, Noah might begin with one evening question he no longer asks his partner or answers internally.

He will still notice other reassurance patterns.

He does not need to turn the first week into an impossible total ban in order for the practice to count.

What to do with the unanswered question

After refusing reassurance, the mind may shout the question more loudly.

Do not replace the answer with a new answer.

Return to behavior.

Stand up and finish the dishes.

Continue the conversation.

Read the next page.

Walk to the train.

The ordinary action is not evidence that everything is safe.

It is evidence only that you can continue without another verdict.

Reassurance that sounds like education

A common online pattern is reading "just one more" explanation.

The person is not asking, "Am I safe?"

They are asking, "Can you explain the mechanism again?"

The distinction can be real. Learning needs repetition sometimes.

But watch the timing.

If the request appears exactly when anxiety spikes, if the same concept has already been understood, and if the answer is judged by whether relief arrives, education may be functioning as reassurance.

Try an experiment.

Choose one concept you already understand, such as the definition of a mental compulsion.

Do not reread it during the next spike.

Use the skill you already have.

If a genuine learning question remains later, return to it during a planned study time.

This separates education from emergency certainty seeking.

It also protects books, podcasts, forums, and therapy notes from becoming a library of reassurance objects.

Principles to Remember

Reassurance can happen with no other person present. Silent evidence, remembered statements, and internal verdicts can serve the same certainty function as repeated questions to someone else.

Information and reassurance are not separated by topic. Ask whether the answer is needed for a real action or whether it is being repeated because confidence has fallen.

A non-engagement response does not need to prove that the fear is irrational. It only needs to decline the next certainty procedure.

Chapter 7: The Feeling Check

Mei does not ask, "Am I attracted to him?"

She looks.

That difference makes the ritual hard to recognize.

She glances at a photo of her partner and turns attention inward. Is there warmth? Excitement? A physical response? She notices almost nothing. Anxiety rises.

She looks again, this time at a favorite picture from a vacation.

A little warmth appears.

Relief arrives, then suspicion: *Did I manufacture that because I wanted to pass the test?*

She checks again.

When a feeling becomes evidence

A **feeling check** is monitoring an internal state in order to use that state as evidence.

The target can be attraction, guilt, disgust, certainty, anxiety, sincerity, arousal, love, anger, fear, or a sense that something feels "right."

Internal states are real. Paying attention to them is not automatically compulsive.

The problem is repeated measurement for a verdict.

Ben has a moral obsession and checks whether he feels guilty enough. If guilt is strong, he is briefly relieved because "a bad person would not care." Then he worries that the relief proves selfishness.

Marcus checks whether his chest feels normal. The act of monitoring produces more sensations to interpret.

Aisha checks whether a prayer feels sincere. The closer she listens, the less certain sincerity feels.

Attention changes the test

When you repeatedly inspect an internal state, the inspection itself becomes part of the experience.

Try a harmless example. Notice how your tongue sits in your mouth. You probably were not concerned with it ten seconds ago. Now the sensation is prominent.

Or monitor whether your breathing feels automatic. The act of watching can make breathing feel less automatic.

This does not prove that every feeling check creates a false sensation. It shows why internal state is a poor laboratory when the observer is also changing attention, expectation, and anxiety.

The more important clinical point is functional: ERP does not require you to obtain the correct internal feeling before you continue. Response prevention often means allowing the feeling to remain ambiguous.

The "right feeling" compulsion

Some compulsions are driven less by a feared catastrophe than by incompleteness or a sense that something is not right.

A person rereads a sentence until it sounds right.

Another repeats a name until it feels clean.

Another replays an apology until it feels sincere.

Another checks a memory until the emotional tone matches what they believe they should feel.

OCD presentations can include "just right" experiences and incompleteness concerns, which have been documented in clinical research (Sibrava et al., 2016).

For covert rituals, the practical risk is that "rightness" becomes the stopping rule.

If the exercise ends only when the internal click arrives, the feeling is controlling behavior.

Feeling is not a verdict

Consider attraction.

Attraction naturally varies with mood, fatigue, context, conflict, attention, stress, and many other factors. It is not a courtroom test that can answer every relationship question.

Consider guilt.

Guilt can be appropriate, excessive, absent, delayed, or mixed. Measuring guilt repeatedly does not establish moral truth.

Consider anxiety.

Low anxiety during an exposure does not prove the exercise failed. High anxiety does not prove it worked. Modern exposure models place less emphasis on waiting for fear to decline within a session and more on new learning that can compete with old threat expectations (Craske et al., 2014; Craske et al., 2022).

That shift is useful for covert OCD because it removes one more internal score.

You do not have to make yourself feel uncertain enough, anxious enough, or calm enough.

You practice the chosen behavior while the feelings do whatever they do.

The mirror-check equivalent

Physical checking is easy to picture. Someone looks in the mirror, inspects a lock, or examines a body part.

Feeling checking is the internal equivalent.

The “mirror” is attention.

You point it inward and ask for evidence.

One check often produces ambiguity, which triggers a second.

Recognizing that structure can help you stop treating the ritual as passive self-awareness.

Choose one state not to score

Pick one internal state that you repeatedly measure.

For one day, do not assign it a number, verdict, or comparison.

You may notice the feeling automatically. You may even notice yourself checking before you can stop.

When you recognize the check, leave the result uninterpreted.

Instead of “I felt only three out of ten attraction, so this means…,” stop after “I noticed myself measuring.”

Return to the external activity.

If a genuine decision about your life needs attention, schedule that decision for a reasonable time and use broader evidence than a momentary internal reading.

When tracking is clinically useful

Therapy sometimes uses ratings. A clinician may ask about distress, urges, or symptom frequency to plan treatment.

That does not make all ratings compulsive.

The difference is purpose and schedule.

A planned rating completed once for treatment can be data. Repeating the rating every two minutes to see whether anxiety is falling is recovery checking.

If you work with a clinician, follow the agreed measurement plan. Do not add extra measurements because the official one feels uncertain.

Checking certainty about OCD itself

Feeling checks can attach to the diagnosis.

"Do I feel like this is OCD?"

"Am I distressed enough for it to count?"

"Does this thought feel ego-dystonic enough?"

"Do I feel relieved by reassurance, and if I do, does that prove OCD?"

These questions turn internal state into diagnostic evidence.

Diagnosis should not be made by repeatedly measuring a feeling.

If you need diagnostic clarification, bring the pattern to a qualified professional. Then use the treatment plan rather than constantly re-diagnosing yourself from moment to moment.

Testing attraction, arousal, and identity

Some covert OCD themes involve sexuality, attraction, or identity. These areas deserve careful language because ordinary exploration can be healthy and meaningful.

A feeling check is not defined by the topic.

It is defined by repeated monitoring for certainty.

A person can reflect on identity without OCD.

A person with OCD can also repeatedly test reactions to images, people, words, or bodily sensations in order to obtain a definitive internal verdict.

The test itself can change attention and arousal, which then creates more material to interpret.

Do not use this book to decide anyone's identity.

Use it to notice whether repetitive testing has become the response to uncertainty.

A clinician familiar with both OCD and respectful identity-affirming care can help when the distinction is hard.

Moral feeling checks

Ben's ritual is built around guilt.

He believes a good person would feel a specific amount of remorse after an intrusive thought.

So he checks.

If guilt is present, he is temporarily reassured.

If it fades, he becomes alarmed.

This turns emotion into a morality meter.

But emotions are influenced by fatigue, repetition, attention, context, and many other variables. An internal reading cannot carry the entire burden of ethical judgment.

Ethics are expressed through choices and behavior.

You do not need a perfect feeling before making a responsible choice.

The rebound check

Sometimes a reader stops checking one feeling and starts checking whether they are checking.

"Was that a check?"

"Did I look inward for too long?"

"Did I accidentally test?"

That is recovery checking.

Use the gray-zone rule from Chapter 2.

If you cannot classify the last three seconds quickly, leave them unclassified.

Return to the external task.

The treatment is not improved by putting every moment on trial.

A wider field of attention

One practical way to reduce feeling checks is not to force attention outward but to widen it.

You may notice attraction, anxiety, or guilt while also noticing the room, the conversation, the task, and the other person's words.

The internal state does not have to disappear.

It simply loses its job as the only data source that matters.

This is not a special meditation exercise.

It is a reminder that life contains more than the instrument panel inside your body.

Feeling checks in relationships

Relationship uncertainty makes feeling checks especially seductive because people are taught to "listen to your feelings."

That advice is not wrong.

It is incomplete when someone has a compulsive checking pattern.

A relationship decision can include emotion, values, behavior, compatibility, safety, and practical realities.

It does not have to be decided by a momentary internal scan repeated twenty times per day.

Elena chooses a weekly time to reflect on an actual relationship concern with her therapist.

Outside that window, she notices the urge to check whether she "feels in love."

She does not forbid feelings.

She stops turning each feeling into a referendum.

This creates space for a broader decision process.

If a relationship is unsafe, abusive, or coercive, the issue is not an OCD exposure target. Seek appropriate support.

Response prevention should never be used to keep someone in danger or to dismiss concrete evidence of mistreatment.

In a Nutshell

A feeling check turns an internal state into a verdict machine. The state can be attraction, guilt, disgust, anxiety, sincerity, certainty, or "rightness."

Attention can change what you notice, and repeated measurement creates more material to interpret. ERP does not require a correct feeling before action.

Practice leaving one internal reading unscored. Notice the check, decline the interpretation, and return to what you were doing.

Chapter 8: Neutralizing in Disguise

Maya learned a calming exercise years before she understood her OCD.

Whenever an unwanted image appeared, she replaced it with a safe image. If she pictured a car accident, she immediately imagined everyone stepping out unharmed. If she had a blasphemous thought, she pictured a peaceful place. If a violent word appeared, she mentally substituted a kind one.

The replacement felt healthy because it was gentle.

It was also compulsory.

Maya had built a rule: bad mental content could not remain uncorrected.

A strategy can change jobs

Neutralizing is any mental act used to cancel, correct, balance, or make another mental event feel safer.

The act might be a phrase, image, prayer, number, memory, or opposite thought.

The content can look positive.

That is why function matters again.

A grounding exercise used at a planned time to reconnect with the present is not automatically a compulsion. The same exercise performed every time an intrusive thought appears because the thought must be removed can become part of the ritual.

A prayer offered as part of faith is not automatically a compulsion. The same prayer repeated until it feels perfectly sincere or until a feared thought feels canceled may be serving a compulsive function.

Mindfulness is not automatically a compulsion. But "being mindful" can become a covert demand to achieve a clean, detached mental state before continuing.

No technique has permanent immunity.

The healthy-tool trap

People who have read a lot about anxiety can accumulate tools.

Label the thought.

Breathe.

Defuse.

Reframe.

Accept.

Name five things.

Repeat a compassionate statement.

Each can have a legitimate use.

Then OCD asks a new question: *Did you use the tool correctly enough to make this safe?*

You label the thought "OCD" five times.

You repeat an acceptance phrase until anxiety shifts.

You breathe while checking whether the unwanted image is fading.

You remind yourself that thoughts are not actions, not to learn the concept, but to obtain certainty about your own thought.

The tool has crossed the Answering Line.

Thought replacement

One of the clearest neutralizing patterns is replacement.

An unwanted thought appears.

You deliberately generate its opposite.

The immediate aim is to make the original less dangerous, less offensive, or less predictive.

The problem is not that positive imagery is forbidden. The problem is the rule that every disturbing mental event requires correction.

Response prevention breaks that rule by allowing the original thought to remain uncorrected.

That can feel irresponsible when the content is moral, religious, or violent. The exposure is not endorsement. It is a decision not to perform a private cancellation ceremony.

Thought content and intention are not identical. Clinical descriptions of OCD recognize unwanted aggressive, sexual, religious, and other taboo obsessions, and do not treat the mere presence of those thoughts as behavior (NIMH, 2023).

Prayer and moral practice

This area needs care.

A book should not tell you what your faith requires.

If prayer, confession, reflection, or moral examination is part of your tradition, speak with a trusted religious leader who understands OCD if you need help separating ordinary practice from compulsive repetition. An OCD-trained clinician can also help with the behavioral pattern.

Aisha's issue is not that she prays.

It is that she repeats a prayer until the internal sense of sincerity reaches a threshold, then restarts if a distracting thought appears.

Her ERP target might be the repetition, not the practice itself.

Ordinary religious observance remains.

The certainty ritual does not have to.

Counting, symmetry, and mental balancing

Neutralizing can be nonverbal.

A person counts to a safe number after a feared thought.

Another imagines equal shapes on both sides of an image.

Another mentally "undoes" a movement by picturing it backward.

Another pairs a feared name with a safe name.

These acts can be fast and highly practiced. They may not feel like choices at first.

Use the same sequence from Chapter 3: signal, urge, added response.

You are not responsible for preventing the signal.

You can begin to experiment with not completing the added response.

The function audit

Choose three coping strategies you use often.

For each, ask:

1. What is the intended skill?
2. When do I use it?
3. What do I demand that it change inside me?
4. Do I repeat it if the internal change does not happen?
5. Would I still use it if it did not reduce uncertainty today?

That fifth question is especially useful.

If you would abandon the tool the moment it failed to lower distress, its current job may be symptom control rather than flexible practice.

This does not mean the tool is bad.

It means you may need to change how you use it.

When "maybe" becomes a ritual

A classic ERP-style response is "maybe, maybe not."

It can be useful because it does not resolve the feared question.

It can also become a chant.

If you say it forty times while checking whether uncertainty feels acceptable, the phrase is now serving a control function.

Use responses lightly.

One sentence.

Then behavior.

The ordinary action after the phrase is more important than the phrase itself.

When coping becomes compulsory

A coping strategy is flexible when you can choose whether to use it.

A compulsion is governed by a rule.

"I must do this after that thought."

"I cannot continue until the phrase feels right."

"I need to complete the breathing pattern before I speak."

"I have to label the thought correctly."

Watch for the word **must** in your private treatment routine.

Sometimes “must” reflects ordinary safety or a clinician's instruction.

Often in covert OCD it marks a condition the mind has added to participation.

The problem with counter-thoughts

A counter-thought tries to defeat an obsession with content.

Obsessive thought: “Maybe I am selfish.”

Counter-thought: “I am generous.”

Obsessive thought: “Maybe I will lose control.”

Counter-thought: “I am completely safe.”

Obsessive thought: “Maybe the relationship is wrong.”

Counter-thought: “We are perfect together.”

The counter-thought can bring relief, but it accepts the obsession's premise that a verdict must be produced.

Non-engagement does something different.

It does not counter.

It declines.

Neutralizing through research

Not all neutralizing stays inside the mind.

A person may search for a quotation, statistic, rule, or diagnosis to cancel a feared interpretation.

Then the external information is repeated internally.

The chain moves back and forth across the skull, but the function stays stable.

This is why the book treats visible and invisible rituals as one system.

Stopping the Google search but continuing the remembered argument is incomplete.

Stopping the internal argument but immediately asking a forum may be incomplete too.

Respecting meaningful practices

It is possible to become overzealous and classify every repeated practice as OCD.

People repeat prayers.

Musicians repeat scales.

Athletes repeat drills.

Writers reread sentences.

Parents check on children.

Patients follow monitoring plans.

Meaning and context matter.

Ask whether repetition is proportionate to the ordinary purpose and whether you can stop at a reasonable point despite some uncertainty.

If a practice is central to faith, culture, or health, do not redesign it alone based on a generic rule. Use informed professional or community guidance.

Tool fasting

If one recovery tool has become ritualized, try a short period without that tool, if doing so is safe and does not conflict with treatment instructions.

For example, stop using the phrase "maybe, maybe not" for one evening.

Do not replace it with a different phrase.

Use behavior as the response: notice the urge, then continue the task.

The exercise helps reveal whether the words themselves had become a condition for moving on.

If the tool is part of clinician-guided treatment, discuss the change first.

Mindfulness without a cleanliness rule

Mindfulness language can accidentally create a new standard.

"Observe the thought."

"Let it pass."

"Return to the present."

A reader can interpret those instructions as:

Observe it perfectly.

Make it pass.

Prove you are present.

The repair is simple.

Mindfulness, when used alongside ERP, can support noticing without immediate reaction, but it does not need to erase the thought. IOCDF currently lists mindfulness-based therapy as an adjunctive treatment rather than a replacement for primary OCD treatments and describes it as supporting awareness and acceptance of present thoughts and emotions (IOCDF, n.d.-b).

If you use a mindfulness skill, set a behavioral purpose.

"I am noticing the urge so I can choose not to neutralize."

Then let the exercise be messy.

If the thought sticks around, the practice can still be complete.

If attention wanders, return without grading the return.

The standard is not mental cleanliness.

Principles to Remember

Neutralizing tries to cancel or correct mental content. It can hide inside positive imagery, prayer, counting, mindfulness, labeling, reframing, or other apparently healthy tools.

The tool is not classified by reputation. Ask what job it is doing now.

A response-prevention practice allows unwanted mental content to remain uncorrected while preserving ordinary values, faith, safety, and responsible action.

Chapter 9: Nonengagement Without Suppression

Grace is halfway through a film when an old obsession appears.

The thought is not new. That is part of the frustration. She has answered it before, discussed it in therapy, written about it, and watched it return anyway.

Her first impulse is to push it away.

She focuses hard on the dialogue. The thought comes back.

She tells herself not to think it. The effort makes her check whether she is still thinking it.

She tries to "let it be," then monitors whether she is letting it be correctly.

Within three minutes, every strategy has become another conversation with the thought.

Non-engagement begins where that conversation ends.

What non-engagement is

A **non-engagement response** is a brief choice not to solve, debate, neutralize, verify, or finish an obsessional question, followed by returning attention to a chosen activity.

The definition has two parts.

First, you decline the certainty work.

Second, you do something else that matters in the actual situation.

The second part keeps non-engagement from becoming a staring contest with the thought.

Grace does not need to stand inside her mind and prove that she is refusing well. She can notice the pull to analyze, stop feeding it, and turn back toward the film even if the thought remains audible in the background.

The objective is not absence.

It is nonparticipation in the ritual.

Suppression asks for disappearance

Thought suppression has a different goal.

It says: *This thought must not be here.*

That creates a monitoring problem. In order to know whether the thought is gone, you have to check for it. The act of checking keeps the topic active.

Classic experimental work found paradoxical rebound effects after deliberate thought suppression under the study conditions (Wegner et al., 1987). That does not mean every attempt to redirect attention will produce rebound. The narrower lesson here is that making "I must not think this" the treatment goal can pull attention back toward monitoring whether the thought is present.

ERP already gives you a better target: the compulsion.

You can let the obsession exist without completing the response.

The three moves

Use three moves.

Notice. "There is the question."

Decline. "I am not working that out now."

Return. Resume the next chosen action.

You do not have to speak any of those sentences. They describe a sequence.

Luis notices an intrusive doubt while cooking. He feels the urge to review a conversation. He does not argue with the doubt. He returns to chopping the vegetables.

Thirty seconds later the doubt appears again.

He repeats the behavioral choice.

Not because the first attempt failed.

Because the thought returning is not failure.

The no-secret-answer rule

A non-engagement phrase should not contain a hidden reassurance.

Compare:

"I am not answering whether I offended her."

with:

"I am not answering because I know I probably did not offend her."

The second sentence gives the mind an answer on the way out.

Compare:

"I can leave this medical doubt open until the appointment I already scheduled."

with:

"I can leave it open because the odds are tiny that anything is wrong."

Again, the second sentence sneaks reassurance into the method.

A neutral response does not have to be bleak. It simply refuses to settle the feared content.

Returning is not distraction

People sometimes hear "return to the activity" and assume that means distraction.

The distinction is purpose.

Distraction as a safety behavior says, "I must keep my attention away from the thought so I do not feel distress."

Flexible attention says, "The thought can be present, and I am choosing to use my attention on this task."

If the obsession keeps breaking through, you do not need to win an attention contest.

Read the same sentence twice if needed.

Ask someone to repeat a question at work.

Keep walking even while part of your mind is noisy.

The exposure is learning that the activity does not have to wait for internal closure.

Non-engagement during strong emotion

When distress is intense, short responses are often better.

A long explanation creates more material for debate.

Try one of these:

"Not solving."

"Open question."

"I can act without a verdict."

"Maybe. I am moving on."

Do not search for the perfect phrase. Pick one or use none.

If a phrase begins to feel compulsory, drop it and return through behavior alone.

The difference between emotion regulation and ritual

You are allowed to care for your body.

Eating, sleeping, taking prescribed medication, stretching, taking an ordinary break, and using a clinician-taught regulation skill are not automatically compulsions.

The function test still applies.

Are you using the skill because a human body needs rest, or because the obsession may not remain present during rest?

Are you breathing slowly because your clinician taught you how to manage panic safely, or because you believe the feared thought must disappear before you continue?

The same act can serve more than one function.

Do not classify every comfort as avoidance.

Self-help becomes punitive when it turns normal care into a prohibited behavior.

A five-minute practice

Choose a low-to-moderate trigger that naturally appears.

For five minutes, practice the three moves.

Notice the obsessional question.

Decline analysis once.

Return to one concrete activity.

Each time you catch yourself reviewing or reassuring, stop where you are. Do not rewind the five minutes to make them "clean."

At the end, record only two facts:

Did the trigger show up?

Did you resume the named activity after noticing ritualizing at least once?

Do not grade how accepted, calm, uncertain, or detached you felt.

Those feelings are not the assignment.

When you genuinely need to think

Sometimes you need deliberate reflection.

A relationship decision may deserve an hour. A complex work problem may require research. A medical decision may require consultation.

Use structure.

Choose a time.

Name the decision.

Identify the information source.

Set a stopping rule.

Then stop when the rule is met, even if doubt remains.

This keeps ordinary thinking available while limiting the endless version.

Non-engagement is not passive

The word can sound as if you are supposed to sit still and wait.

In practice, non-engagement is active at the level that matters.

You choose not to open the internal case.

You choose not to add another piece of evidence.

You choose a real-world action.

Luis notices an intrusive question while getting ready for work. He does not have to stand in the hallway "accepting" it for ten minutes. He can put on his coat and leave.

The exposure is carried with him.

The thought may still be present.

His behavior is no longer waiting for a verdict.

The conversation metaphor

Imagine that a person you know asks the same unanswerable question every five minutes.

You might answer once.

Then again.

By the tenth repetition, you realize the problem is not lack of information.

It is the structure of the conversation.

Mental compulsions can work the same way.

The mind asks a new version.

You answer.

It changes one condition.

You answer again.

Non-engagement means recognizing the conversation type.

You do not need a better answer.

You need to stop participating in the repetitive format.

What "return" should look like

The return action should be concrete enough to begin.

"Live my values" is too broad in the middle of a spike.

"Finish washing this plate" is concrete.

"Be present" is too broad.

"Listen to the next sentence my friend says" is concrete.

"Focus on work" is too broad.

"Open the file and write the first line of the report" is concrete.

Small actions give attention somewhere to go without requiring internal silence.

Re-entry is part of the skill

The thought will interrupt again.

When it does, the mind may say, "See, returning did not work."

That assumes the return was supposed to prevent recurrence.

It was not.

Every re-entry is another repetition of the skill.

Notice.

Decline.

Return.

If you do that twenty times in a morning, you did not fail nineteen times.

You practiced twenty times.

When non-engagement feels dishonest

People with moral and relationship obsessions often say, "Ignoring this feels dishonest."

Non-engagement is not pretending the question has no importance.

It is choosing the proper level of response.

If there is a real action, take it.

If no action is available and the remaining work is an attempt to obtain certainty, declining that work is not dishonesty.

You can care about truth without conducting an endless private interrogation.

A phrase audit

Write down the three phrases you use most when intrusive thoughts appear.

For each, ask:

Do I say this once or until I feel different?

Does the phrase answer the feared content?

Do I check whether I "believe" it?

Can I continue my activity without saying it?

If the phrase has become compulsory, shorten it or drop it.

Behavior can carry non-engagement without commentary.

When the mind keeps talking

Non-engagement does not require silence.

Luis practices while making breakfast.

The thought says, *Maybe you said something unforgivable yesterday.*

He notices the urge to review.

He keeps making breakfast.

The mind produces a second sentence: *Avoiding the review proves you do not care.*

He does not answer.

A third sentence appears: *A decent person would at least check.*

He keeps moving.

This can feel strange because the mind is still active. You may assume that if sentences are appearing, you are "engaging."

Not necessarily.

Mental activity is not the same as ritual participation.

The distinction is what you add deliberately.

If an argument appears and you do not take the next step in the argument, the mind can keep generating material without your cooperation.

That may be the most important practical meaning of "let the thought be."

You are not making it disappear.

You are letting it exist without turning it into a task.

In a Nutshell

Non-engagement is not thought control. It is a behavioral decision not to continue the certainty work.

Use notice, decline, return. Keep the response brief. Do not hide reassurance inside the phrase.

Returning attention is not the same as forcing distraction. The thought can remain present while you resume a chosen action.

Chapter 10: Build Response Prevention

A response-prevention plan that says “do not do compulsions” is too vague.

Priya learned that the hard way.

She planned an exposure around making a minor work decision without extra checking. Her rule was that she would not reopen the document after sending it.

She sent the document once.

Then she mentally reread the most important paragraph.

She recalled the numbers.

She imagined what her manager might notice.

She reassured herself that the decision was reasonable.

She did not reopen the file, so part of her still believed she had followed the plan.

The visible compulsion stopped.

The hidden version inherited the job.

Make the target observable to you

Response prevention means refraining from the compulsive response after the obsession or trigger is present. That is the second half of ERP (IOCDF, n.d.-a).

For covert OCD, the target must be described as an action you can recognize.

Bad target: “Do not ruminate.”

Better target: “Do not replay the meeting to determine whether I sounded rude.”

Bad target: "Do not reassure."

Better target: "Do not list reasons that the intrusive thought does not represent my character."

Bad target: "Do not check."

Better target: "Do not scan my body for a specific sensation to decide whether I feel attraction."

The more specific version gives you something to prevent.

Predict the substitute

Before an exposure, ask:

If I could not use my usual ritual, what would I do instead to get the same certainty?

Jonah cannot review the party memory, so he checks guilt.

Mei cannot check attraction, so she compares the relationship with an old one.

Marcus cannot search symptoms, so he repeats his doctor's reassurance.

Aisha cannot repeat a prayer, so she examines whether the first prayer felt sincere.

These substitutions are not evidence that ERP is impossible.

They are information about the ritual function.

Add them to the plan.

Build a response-prevention statement

A useful statement has four parts.

Trigger: What will you contact?

Primary ritual: What will you not do?

Likely substitutes: What related certainty behaviors will you watch for?

Return action: What ordinary activity will you continue or resume?

Example:

"After I send the email, I will not reread it to check tone. I will also not replay the wording from memory, check my anxiety for evidence, or ask a coworker whether it sounded rude. I will begin the next task on my list."

This is not a contract to perform perfectly.

It is a map for recognizing what matters.

Ordinary safety stays

ERP does not require recklessness.

The **ordinary safety** rule is simple: preserve legal, ethical, medical, and practical precautions that would make sense without an OCD demand for extra certainty.

You still stop at red lights.

You still follow medication instructions.

You still wash your hands when ordinary hygiene calls for it.

You still respond to genuine workplace safety procedures.

You still seek medical care for symptoms that meet ordinary clinical guidance.

You do not use "exposure" as a reason to handle dangerous materials, drive unsafely, ignore symptoms a clinician told you to report, or break laws.

Professional ERP guidance describes exposure as planned contact with feared cues and is commonly introduced under clinical guidance, not as deliberate danger (IOCDF, n.d.-a; NIMH, 2023).

When you are unsure whether reducing a behavior is safe, ask a qualified professional.

Harm obsessions and real danger

Intrusive harm thoughts require especially clear boundaries.

If your problem is unwanted harm images and compulsive reassurance, an exposure can involve allowing the thought, reading a safe cue word, writing an imaginal uncertainty statement, or remaining in an ordinary situation without extra reassurance.

It should not involve actual dangerous behavior.

Do not use weapons, unsafe driving, self-injury, dangerous heights, medication misuse, or other genuine hazards as self-directed exposure tasks.

If you have intent, a plan, or concern that you may act on harm toward yourself or someone else, that is not a self-help ERP exercise. Seek immediate professional or emergency help appropriate to your location.

A book cannot assess risk.

Support people and reassurance

Response prevention often affects other people.

Noah's partner has been answering the same reassurance question twenty times a night. A plan that simply says “never answer him again” may produce conflict and leave both people unsure what to do.

A better plan is agreed when the obsession is not peaking.

They decide that Noah can say, “I am having the urge to ask.”

His partner can respond once with support for the plan rather than reassurance about the feared content.

Then the conversation moves to a normal topic or ordinary shared activity.

If Noah asks again, the partner does not need a lecture. A short reminder is enough.

If you are in therapy, build family or partner responses with the clinician.

Response prevention is not endurance theater

Some people think “harder” automatically means “better.”

It does not.

An exposure that is so intense you spend the whole time dissociating, escaping mentally, or planning never to do it again may be poorly designed.

A response-prevention plan that removes every source of comfort, rest, information, and support can become punitive.

The target is the compulsion, not human needs.

Choose work that is challenging enough to contact the obsession and realistic enough to repeat.

Inhibitory-learning approaches to exposure also emphasize varying learning opportunities rather than relying only on a fixed hierarchy or waiting for within-session fear reduction (Craske et al., 2014; Craske et al., 2022).

Intensity is one variable, not the score.

The one-page plan

For one trigger, write:

Trigger.

Primary mental ritual.

Likely substitute mental rituals.

Any visible rituals.

Ordinary safety behavior that stays.

Return action.

Who can support the plan, if anyone.

What would count as genuinely new information requiring a different response.

Keep the page short.

The plan should reduce ambiguity, not become a new document to perfect.

Response prevention needs a hierarchy too

People build exposure hierarchies but sometimes forget that response prevention can be graded.

A person who performs a mental ritual for two hours may not begin by preventing every version for an entire day.

A first step might be delaying the review for ten minutes.

A second might be ending one replay after the first pass.

A third might be leaving one category of evidence unchecked.

The direction is toward fuller response prevention, not permanent partial rituals.

Grading can make the skill repeatable enough to learn.

A clinician can help decide when partial prevention is appropriate and when it risks preserving the loop.

Family accommodation

OCD can recruit family members into rituals.

A partner answers questions.

A parent checks something on the reader's behalf.

A friend listens to repeated reconstructions.

A coworker is asked to proofread work beyond the normal standard.

OCD literature uses the term **family accommodation** for ways relatives participate in rituals, facilitate avoidance, or otherwise change their behavior around symptoms. Research has associated greater accommodation with more severe symptoms and impairment, and family interventions may directly target accommodation alongside ERP (Lebowitz et al., 2012; Thompson-Hollands et al., 2015).

The covert version can be subtle.

You do the mental review privately, then ask another person for one final confirmation.

A response-prevention plan should include that last step.

Define ordinary safety before the spike

It is difficult to decide what counts as “normal” when anxiety is already high.

Set the rule in advance.

For health concerns, use guidance from your actual medical professionals.

For driving, use ordinary laws and procedures.

For work, use established quality standards.

For hygiene, use ordinary public-health practices.

For caregiving, follow real responsibilities.

Then notice the extra behavior added only because certainty feels insufficient.

The advance rule reduces the temptation to renegotiate safety every time OCD produces a new exception.

What not to prevent

Do not prevent behavior merely because it lowers anxiety.

Eating lunch may lower anxiety.

Talking with a friend may lower anxiety.

Rest may lower anxiety.

Taking prescribed medication may lower anxiety.

A useful response-prevention plan targets the behavior because it is part of the obsessive-compulsive cycle, not because relief is forbidden.

This distinction keeps ERP humane and precise.

Prevent the ritual, keep the repair

If you make a real mistake during an exposure, repair it.

Suppose Grace sends an email with the wrong attachment.

She can send the correct attachment.

Response prevention does not require pretending the mistake did not happen.

The target is the additional behavior that tries to erase all uncertainty about what the mistake means.

She can repair the file without replaying her moral character.

That is ordinary responsibility plus response prevention.

A response-prevention plan for mixed rituals

Most real episodes contain more than one ritual.

Jonah's trigger is a memory.

Primary ritual: reconstruct the scene.

Substitute one: check guilt.

Substitute two: compare himself with another person.

Visible ritual: search old messages.

Reassurance route: ask a friend what “someone like that” would remember.

His plan cannot simply say “do not review.”

It needs a small hierarchy of priorities.

First, prevent the main reconstruction.

Second, if a substitute appears, label its function once and stop it.

Third, avoid the most likely external reassurance route for the planned window.

Fourth, return to a specific activity.

If he catches a fourth ritual not listed, he does not need to rewrite the plan immediately.

He can treat it by function.

Response-prevention plans should be detailed enough to guide behavior and simple enough to use while distressed.

If yours takes twenty minutes to read, shorten it.

Principles to Remember

Response prevention works better when the target is specific. Name the mental act, predict substitutes, and decide what ordinary action follows.

Keep ordinary safety. ERP is not dangerous exposure, medical neglect, or moral indifference.

A plan is a map, not a purity test. Catching a substitute late still gives you a chance to stop feeding it.

Chapter 11: Expose the Unanswered Question

There is no contaminated surface in Elena's exposure.

There is no lock to leave unchecked.

There is no appliance to walk away from.

The trigger is a sentence.

Maybe this relationship is wrong for me.

For months Elena tried to build ERP around external situations. She looked at photos of happy couples. She watched romantic films. She went on dates without asking for reassurance.

But the central ritual continued. After every trigger she compared feelings, reviewed conversations, and mentally calculated whether her relationship met the correct standard.

The external exposure was real.

So was the internal escape.

Exposure can be mental

IOCDF's ERP description includes confronting thoughts and images as well as objects and situations (IOCDF, n.d.-a). That matters for covert OCD because the feared cue may be a possibility rather than a physical object.

An exposure can involve:

A word.

A sentence.

An image.

A memory cue.

An ordinary situation that raises uncertainty.

A deliberate decision to leave a question unanswered.

What makes it exposure is planned contact with the feared or uncertain cue.

What makes it ERP is the response prevention that follows.

Start with the feared question

Ask:

What uncertainty does the ritual keep trying to settle?

Not the whole biography. One question.

"Did I offend her?"

"Could this feeling mean I do not love him?"

"Could I have made a serious mistake?"

"Could this symptom mean something bad?"

"Could the intrusive thought say something about me?"

Then build contact with the question without building a verdict.

For Elena, the cue might be reading once: "Maybe I will never know with complete certainty what this relationship will become."

For Grace: "Maybe someone did think my joke was rude."

For Marcus: "This sensation may remain uncertain until ordinary medical care gives me a reason to act."

The wording should be truthful at the level of uncertainty.

It should not exaggerate danger.

Exposure is not confession

People with moral or harm obsessions sometimes turn exposure statements into false confessions.

"I am definitely dangerous."

"I certainly committed the offense."

"I know I am a bad person."

That is not necessary.

Exposure can contact uncertainty without asserting a fact you do not know.

"Maybe."

"It is possible I will not get certainty."

"I cannot prove the feared interpretation is impossible."

The aim is willingness to remain without the ritual, not forcing yourself to make a false claim.

The three-rung uncertainty practice

Build three versions of the same cue.

Rung one: A mild, ordinary cue that brings the question to mind.

Rung two: A clearer statement of the uncertain possibility.

Rung three: A natural situation in which the same uncertainty matters more.

Example for Grace:

Rung one: Read the sentence, "People sometimes misunderstand jokes."

Rung two: Read once, "Maybe my coworker disliked what I said, and I may not know."

Rung three: Attend a meeting, speak normally, and resist reviewing afterward.

The ladder is not a race.

If Rung two reveals a hidden ritual you had missed, stay there long enough to learn the response-prevention skill.

How long should exposure last

There is no single number that fits every exposure.

Older exposure practice often emphasized remaining in the situation until anxiety declined. Contemporary inhibitory-learning models argue that fear reduction during the exercise is not the only or necessary marker of useful learning; expectancy violation, variability, and retrieval across contexts can matter (Craske et al., 2014; Craske et al., 2022).

For self-directed practice, use a simpler rule:

Stay with the planned cue for the planned period or natural task.

Do not end solely because anxiety rises.

Do not extend solely because anxiety has not fallen.

End according to the plan, then continue response prevention afterward.

A clinician can help tailor duration.

Do not chase uncertainty as a feeling

A strange treatment ritual appears when the reader asks, "Do I feel uncertain enough?"

That is another feeling check.

You do not need to generate a dramatic state of doubt.

You need to stop doing the behavior that was supposed to remove doubt.

Sometimes an exposure feels flat. That can still be useful practice if the response-prevention target is present.

Sometimes it feels intense. Intensity is not proof of correctness.

Behavior first.

Naturalistic exposure

Many covert exposures already happen during the day.

A friend pauses before replying.

A headline contains a feared word.

You notice a bodily sensation.

A memory appears.

Your partner seems distracted.

You make a decision without complete information.

Naturalistic ERP uses those moments rather than manufacturing all triggers.

The sequence is:

Recognize the cue.

Identify the ritual urge.

Prevent the named ritual.

Continue the real task.

This can be more transferable than creating a separate "therapy hour" for every obsession.

The response-prevention window

Plan what happens after exposure.

If you read a feared sentence for two minutes and then spend forty minutes proving it is harmless, the ritual has simply been delayed.

Choose a post-exposure window.

For the next thirty minutes, for example, do not review the exposure, ask whether it worked, compare anxiety, seek reassurance, or research the feared content.

Do normal activities.

If genuinely new information appears, respond to the new information at ordinary standards.

The window gives delayed rituals a clear boundary.

A first exposure

Choose a low-to-moderate question.

Write one uncertainty statement that does not reassure or exaggerate.

Read it once or a few planned times.

For five to ten minutes, refrain from the main mental ritual.

Continue an ordinary activity.

At the end, record only whether you performed the target ritual and whether you returned to the activity.

If the exercise brings severe distress, confusion about safety, or a strong urge to design more extreme tasks, stop self-directed escalation and seek professional help.

Exposure versus testing

Testing looks like exposure from the outside.

You deliberately bring up the feared thought.

You monitor your reaction.

You use the reaction as evidence.

Mei looks at a photo to "expose herself" to relationship doubt, but the real question is whether she feels enough attraction.

The picture has become a test.

An exposure does not ask your internal state to certify the answer.

It asks you to contact the cue while preventing the ritual.

The difference can be one sentence in the plan:

Testing: “Look at the photo and see how I feel.”

Exposure: “Look at the photo, allow whatever feeling appears, and do not measure attraction.”

Exposure versus reassurance rehearsal

A statement can also disguise reassurance.

“Maybe I am safe because this is probably OCD.”

That is not uncertainty.

It gives an answer.

A cleaner exposure statement removes the explanation:

“Maybe I will not get certainty about this today.”

The phrase is less clever.

That is a strength.

Exposure versus punishment

Some people choose harsh content because they believe suffering proves commitment.

They write the most catastrophic script.

They repeat it for hours.

They forbid themselves every comfort.

ERP is not self-punishment.

The goal is learning to respond differently to fear and uncertainty.

An exposure should be connected to the compulsion you want to reduce.

Pain for its own sake is not a treatment principle.

The role of prediction

Before an exposure, write one prediction about behavior rather than emotion.

"If I do not review the meeting, I predict I will feel unable to move on."

"If I send after one proofread, I predict I will want to reopen the message."

"If I do not self-reassure, I predict the doubt will keep demanding an answer."

Then observe what happened.

Maybe the urge stayed strong.

Maybe it rose and fell.

Maybe it returned later.

The learning is not limited to whether the feared catastrophe occurred.

You are learning what happens when the ritual is absent.

Context variation in practice

If one exposure is working, change one feature.

Time of day.

Location.

Wording.

Social context.

Order.

This can make the new response less dependent on a single ritualized setup.

Do not vary everything at once.

The purpose is flexible learning, not confusion.

The first three exercises

Your first three self-directed exposures can follow this pattern:

Exercise one: A mild natural trigger. Prevent one named covert ritual for five minutes.

Exercise two: A short verbal cue. Prevent the main ritual and one common substitute for ten minutes.

Exercise three: An ordinary real-life action that you usually delay for certainty. Complete it at the normal standard and prevent post-event review for a defined window.

Keep the tasks safe and repeatable.

Escalate based on learning, not on pride.

Exposure in conversation

Some of the strongest covert exposures are interpersonal.

Keisha wants to ask a friend whether a comment sounded offensive.

Instead, she stays in the conversation without asking.

That is exposure to social uncertainty plus response prevention.

Later, the friend gives genuine feedback about something unrelated.

Keisha notices the urge to treat the feedback as evidence about the original fear.

She declines the link.

Naturalistic exposure often has these layers.

You contact one uncertainty, then ordinary life produces more information that the mind wants to recruit into the case.

The plan should not make you rigid.

If the friend actually says, "That earlier comment hurt me," respond to the real feedback.

Apologize or clarify as appropriate.

ERP is not refusing evidence.

It is refusing endless speculation when evidence is absent or the practical response is already complete.

In a Nutshell

Covert ERP does not require an external object. Exposure can contact a thought, image, memory, sentence, or uncertain possibility.

Start with the question the ritual is trying to settle. Use truthful uncertainty, not false confession. Pair the cue with specific response prevention.

Do not grade exposure by how uncertain, anxious, or calm you feel. Plan the period after the exercise so delayed review does not become the escape route.

Chapter 12: Use Imaginal Exposure Carefully

Sofia's fear is about a future she cannot test.

She worries that she will stay in her relationship for years, discover she never loved her partner "correctly," and realize she wasted both of their lives.

No real-world exposure can prove or disprove that future today.

She has tried imagining a breakup, but she uses the image as a test. If she feels devastated, that proves love. If she feels relief, it proves the opposite.

The imagination is not yet exposure.

It is a feeling laboratory.

Imaginal exposure uses imagination differently.

What imaginal exposure is for

Imaginal exposure is a structured way to contact feared meaning when direct real-world exposure is impossible, inappropriate, or incomplete.

It may be useful when the fear concerns a future catastrophe, an uncertain past event, a taboo possibility, responsibility, or a consequence that cannot be safely recreated.

Clinical ERP guidance includes imaginal exposure for feared consequences that cannot be reproduced directly or appropriately in real life (Gillihan et al., 2012; Hezel & Simpson, 2019).

The purpose is not to predict the future.

It is not to prove that the feared outcome will occur.

It is not to reassure yourself that you could handle everything.

It is to contact the uncertainty or feared meaning while preventing the ritual used to neutralize it.

Scripts can become reassurance stories

A common mistake is to write an imaginal script with a comforting ending.

"Maybe I made a mistake, but everyone will understand and I will learn from it."

That may be a useful compassionate reflection in another context.

As an OCD exposure, it can close the question too neatly.

Another mistake is catastrophe theater.

"I will certainly lose everything, everyone will hate me, and my life will be ruined."

That asserts a future as fact and can turn exposure into self-punishment.

A better script stays near the actual uncertainty:

"I may never get complete certainty about what happened. It is possible I made a mistake. If new facts require action, I can respond then. Right now I am not reopening the memory to prove what did or did not happen."

Notice the last sentence.

It sets response prevention without reassuring the feared content.

Keep it short

Long scripts can create more places to ritualize.

A person spends an hour making the wording perfect.

They add every feared detail.

They check whether each sentence produces the right amount of anxiety.

They revise until the script feels "real."

Now writing the exposure has become its own compulsion.

For many covert fears, a paragraph or a few sentences are enough.

The exposure is not the literary quality.

It is the willingness to contact the cue without doing the usual certainty work.

Repetition with a purpose

Imaginal exposure is often repeated.

Repetition can help create multiple opportunities to meet the cue without ritualizing. But repetition should be planned, not driven by a need to reach a specific emotional result.

Decide in advance how many reads or how many minutes.

Then stop according to the plan.

If the mind says, "One more time because that last reading did not feel genuine," recognize the familiar "just right" rule.

That extra repetition may be the ritual.

Safety exclusions

Imaginal exposure is mental, but safety still matters.

Do not use this book to design exposure around active suicidal intent, active intent to harm another person, psychosis, severe trauma symptoms that destabilize you, or any situation in which you cannot reliably distinguish an intrusive fear from a plan you may act on.

Seek qualified professional assessment.

Do not pair imaginal exposure with real dangerous acts.

For harm OCD, a clinician may use carefully chosen words, images, or scenarios. That is very different from handling a weapon unsafely, driving recklessly, or placing someone at risk.

For health OCD, imaginal work does not replace medically indicated testing or treatment.

For religious or moral fears, respect ordinary practice and consider collaboration with an informed faith leader when the boundary is unclear.

The uncertainty paragraph

Write three to five sentences.

Sentence one names the uncertainty.

Sentence two allows the feared possibility without claiming it as fact.

Sentence three names what cannot be known now.

Sentence four, if useful, states the response-prevention choice.

Example:

“I may not know exactly what my coworker thought of my comment. It is possible she disliked it. I cannot reconstruct another person's private reaction from memory. I am not replaying the meeting to get certainty.”

Read it once.

Notice the urge to soften it.

Notice the urge to make it harsher.

Leave it as written.

Return to the day.

When to use a clinician

Self-directed imaginal exposure is not the right tool for every reader.

Professional help is especially useful when you are unsure whether the target is OCD, when trauma and OCD overlap, when depression is severe, when compulsions consume many hours, when you cannot maintain ordinary safety, or when previous exposure attempts have become overwhelming.

IOCDF advises that ERP is initially developed and practiced with trained clinical guidance, with self-directed exercises learned over time (IOCDF, n.d.-a).

A skilled clinician can also catch covert rituals that are hard to see from inside the loop.

Imaginal exposure for uncertain memories

An uncertain past event is a common reason to reach for imagery.

The risk is that imagery becomes another reconstruction.

Jonah writes a script about the college party.

If he tries to make the scene accurate, the exercise turns into review.

A better target is the uncertainty:

"I may not get a complete record of that night. There may be details I do not remember. If real information ever appears, I can respond to it. I am not using imagination to reconstruct the missing pieces now."

The exposure contacts not knowing.

It does not invent a history.

Imaginal exposure for future fears

Future fears can also become prediction exercises.

Sofia imagines her relationship ending and checks whether the image makes her sad.

That is a feeling check.

A cleaner imaginal exercise might focus on the possibility that she cannot know the future:

"I may make choices with incomplete information. I could someday regret a decision. I do not get to solve that future from this chair today."

Then she prevents comparison and feeling tests.

The point is not the breakup story.

It is the uncertainty about choosing.

Audio recordings

Some clinicians use recorded imaginal scripts so a person can listen repeatedly without rewriting them.

A recording can be useful.

It can also become ritualized if the reader changes volume, pacing, wording, or number of plays until the exposure feels exactly right.

If you use audio under a clinician's plan, decide the schedule in advance.

Do not add extra plays because the last one felt "wrong."

For self-directed work, written or spoken cues are often enough.

Writing without literary detail

You do not need graphic detail to make imaginal exposure legitimate.

Specificity should serve the feared meaning.

If the fear is "I could be responsible and never know for sure," the script does not need pages of catastrophe.

If the fear is "My relationship may not give me certainty," the script does not need a detailed breakup scene.

Too much detail can make the exercise harder to repeat and easier to ritualize.

Write only what is needed to contact the relevant uncertainty.

Debrief without reassurance

After imaginal exposure, a debrief can easily become a safety conversation.

Instead of asking, "Did this prove the fear is irrational?" ask behavioral questions:

Did I contact the planned cue?

Which ritual urge was strongest?

Did I notice a substitute?

What ordinary action did I return to?

What one change would make the next practice clearer?

Then stop.

The debrief should improve the method, not settle the obsession.

Scripts for moral uncertainty

Moral concerns can make imaginal work feel dangerous.

A reader may fear that writing a possibility is equivalent to endorsing it.

Keep the distinction between statement and action.

"Maybe I made a mistake" is not a confession.

"Maybe I cannot get perfect certainty about my motive" is not approval of harm.

An exposure statement describes uncertainty.

Ordinary ethical action remains available.

If you know you harmed someone, address it.

If you are unsure whether a real-world responsibility exists, use normal standards or seek appropriate advice.

Then avoid converting moral concern into hours of private prosecution.

A clinician who understands scrupulosity can be especially helpful when religious, moral, or legal duties are hard to distinguish from compulsive rules.

Principles to Remember

Imaginal exposure contacts feared meaning when a safe real-world exposure cannot do so directly. It does not predict the future or require false confessions.

Keep scripts short. Avoid comforting endings and catastrophe theater. Repeat according to a plan, not until the feeling is right.

High-risk, diagnostically unclear, or destabilizing situations need professional assessment rather than self-designed escalation.

Chapter 13: Practice Uncertainty on Purpose

Grace sends the email.

That sentence sounds too ordinary to be an exposure, which is exactly why it matters.

She has written a short update to a coworker. Before treatment, she would read it four or five times, listen to the tone in her head, remove any sentence that might be misunderstood, send it, then reconstruct it from memory while waiting for a reply.

Today she reads it once for obvious errors and sends it.

The uncertainty is small but immediate.

Maybe it sounded curt.

Maybe there was a typo.

Maybe the coworker will read the period at the end of a sentence as irritation.

Grace does not try to feel brave. She opens the next work item.

Uncertainty is not a performance

People sometimes turn acceptance of uncertainty into another internal state to achieve.

They tell themselves, "I should feel open."

Then they check for openness.

They tell themselves, "I should be willing."

Then they measure willingness.

They repeat *maybe, maybe not* until uncertainty feels clean and deliberate.

The exercise becomes a feeling check.

A more useful definition is behavioral: **you act without obtaining the extra certainty the ritual usually demands.**

You can do that while hating the uncertainty.

You can do it while anxious.

You can do it while wondering whether you are doing it correctly.

The behavior is the practice.

Do not manufacture doubt

Another trap is trying to make yourself maximally uncertain.

If you know you turned off the stove because you watched yourself do it once, ERP does not require pretending you have no memory.

If a doctor gives you a clear diagnosis, ERP does not require acting as though you have no medical information.

If your partner directly tells you what they want, you do not need to erase the conversation.

The target is **extra certainty seeking**, not accurate knowledge.

You can know what you reasonably know and still leave the final margin open.

This distinction protects ERP from becoming a contest in self-doubt.

Expectancy and learning

One reason exposure can be useful is that it creates opportunities to learn something different from the rule that fear or uncertainty requires ritual.

Inhibitory-learning models describe exposure as building new learning that can compete with older threat associations rather than simply deleting them. They emphasize expectancy violation, variability, and retrieval of new learning across contexts (Craske et al., 2014; Craske et al., 2022).

You do not need to turn this into neuroscience homework.

A practical version is enough:

"What did I predict I had to do?"

"What happened when I did something different?"

Grace predicted that she had to reread until the email felt safe.

She sent after one ordinary proofread.

The coworker's response is not the only learning outcome. Even if the coworker dislikes the email, Grace has learned that she can tolerate the period before she knows and respond to real feedback if it comes.

That is more durable than proving every email harmless.

Vary the context

A skill learned only in one carefully controlled exercise may stay attached to that setting.

Practice the same response-prevention principle in different places and times.

If your ritual is silent reassurance, practice declining it after a natural trigger at home, then after a mild trigger at work, then during a planned exposure.

If your ritual is mental review, practice leaving one conversation unreconstructed, then one email, then one low-stakes memory.

Variation should not mean random escalation.

It means letting the new response become portable.

Values without turning them into proof

Values can help choose what to do after you decline the ritual.

You might value being present with your children, doing careful work, participating in faith, maintaining friendships, or resting when tired.

The useful question is: “What action fits that value now?”

The dangerous question is: “Does choosing this action prove I am a good person?”

Values are directions.

They are not certificates.

If you use a valued action to prove identity, the action can become another reassurance device.

One ordinary action before you feel finished

Choose something you delay until the mind feels settled.

Send the routine message after one normal check.

Leave the house after the ordinary safety check.

Return to a conversation without replaying your last sentence.

Finish a meal without checking whether an intrusive image has disappeared.

Go to bed without completing one last moral review.

Pick a low-to-moderate target.

Do the ordinary action while the internal sense of incompletion remains.

Then resist the urge to grade the exercise.

The outcome problem

ERP can become secretly outcome-dependent.

“If nothing bad happens, I will know the exposure worked.”

But no exposure can prove that bad outcomes never happen. Ordinary life includes mistakes, misunderstandings, illness, rejection, and regret.

The stronger learning is not “nothing bad ever happens.”

It is “I do not need a ritual to live responsibly under uncertainty.”

That principle survives real life.

The uncertainty budget

You do not have to choose the hardest uncertainty available.

Think about a normal day. You already tolerate thousands of small unknowns.

You send a message without knowing exactly when it will be read.

You eat food without laboratory-testing every ingredient.

You cross a street using ordinary observation rather than proving no driver could make an error.

You accept that another person may misunderstand a sentence.

These are not heroic acts.

They are ordinary life.

OCD often creates a separate standard for one feared domain. In that domain, the normal margin of uncertainty suddenly feels unacceptable.

Practice can begin by restoring the ordinary standard rather than manufacturing extreme doubt.

Stop using relief as the reward

After successful response prevention, relief sometimes arrives.

Enjoying relief is not a problem.

Chasing it is.

If you begin measuring whether anxiety has fallen enough to prove the exercise worked, relief becomes a score.

If you repeat the exposure until the good feeling arrives, the exercise can become another ritual.

Let relief come or not come.

The reward is participation.

Grace's reward is not "I felt calm after sending the email."

It is "I sent the email and did the next task."

The ordinary-risk question

When OCD says, "But what if this really matters?" ask what level of uncertainty other reasonable people accept in the same situation.

This is not an invitation to poll five friends for reassurance.

Use established norms you already know.

A driver follows traffic law.

A patient follows medical guidance.

An employee follows quality procedures.

A parent follows ordinary safety practices.

Once you have the norm, do not repeatedly re-check what "normal people" would do.

That would turn the comparison into reassurance.

Variation without escalation

Variation means changing context.

Escalation means increasing difficulty.

They are not the same.

You can practice leaving an email unreconstructed at work, at home, or on your phone without making the content more frightening.

You can practice silent-reassurance prevention with different mild triggers.

This helps the skill generalize without turning every week into a competition for bigger fear.

A values check that stays behavioral

Ask, “What kind of action do I want to take in the next ten minutes?”

Not, “What kind of person does this prove I am?”

If you value friendship, send the normal message or listen during the conversation.

If you value work, complete the task to the actual standard.

If you value rest, go to bed without finishing the mental review.

The value points toward behavior.

The behavior does not certify identity.

A seven-day experiment

For one week, choose one small daily act that you commonly delay for certainty.

Keep it the same or closely related.

Record only whether you completed the act at the ordinary standard and whether you noticed the main ritual.

Do not record anxiety unless a clinician asked you to.

At the end of the week, ask one question: "What became easier to do?"

That question keeps the focus on life rather than on internal purity.

Uncertainty and real bad outcomes

An exposure does not earn its value only when nothing bad happens.

Grace sends an email after one ordinary proofread.

The next day her manager asks her to correct a typo.

If Grace interprets the typo as proof that response prevention was reckless, she may return to ten checks per email.

A more accurate lesson is narrower.

One ordinary check does not eliminate every error.

Neither do ten checks.

Work systems have repair procedures because mistakes occur.

Grace fixes the typo.

Then she resists the urge to reconstruct the entire decision and prove she was not irresponsible.

ERP has to survive real imperfection or it will collapse the first time life behaves like life.

In a Nutshell

Practicing uncertainty means acting without the extra certainty your ritual usually demands. It does not require manufacturing doubt or achieving a special feeling of acceptance.

Use varied, ordinary situations. Let values point toward action without turning them into identity proof.

The strongest practice is often small: do the next ordinary thing before your mind feels finished.

Chapter 14: When ERP Seems Stuck

Ben has a perfect exposure spreadsheet.

Every exercise is dated.

Every anxiety rating is recorded.

Every target is color-coded.

Every session has a note explaining what he learned.

He is also spending nearly an hour after each exposure determining whether it counted.

His treatment has become the newest place where OCD asks for certainty.

"Stuck" does not always mean the exposure needs to be harder.

Sometimes it means a ritual is hiding inside the method.

First investigate the response

When an exercise seems ineffective, ask these questions before increasing intensity.

What was the target compulsion?

Did a covert version replace it?

Did I reassure myself during the exposure?

Did I review the exposure afterward?

Did I avoid the most relevant cue while technically completing the task?

Did I monitor anxiety or "acceptance" so closely that the measurement became a ritual?

Did I add safety behavior that was not part of ordinary safety?

Gillihan and colleagues' discussion of ERP pitfalls includes missed mental compulsions among the problems that can interfere with treatment (Gillihan et al., 2012).

For this reader, that is often the first place to look.

The "perfect exposure" ritual

Mei plans to look at a photo of her partner without checking attraction.

She does the exercise.

Halfway through, she notices she checked once.

She concludes the exposure is contaminated.

So she starts over.

On the second attempt she notices an automatic body sensation and cannot determine whether she inspected it deliberately.

She starts over again.

Soon the real compulsion is no longer attraction checking.

It is purity checking about ERP.

Use a different standard.

If you notice ritualizing, stop the ritual where you are and continue the planned exposure.

Do not erase the attempt.

Recovery practice includes recovering from the ritual you already started.

Anxiety tracking can become recovery checking

Ratings can be clinically useful. They can help a therapist understand severity, plan a hierarchy, or monitor progress.

But the same rating can become compulsive when it is repeated to answer, “Is this working?”

Ben checks his distress every minute.

If it falls, he worries the exposure was too easy.

If it stays high, he worries he is not learning.

If it rises, he worries he did something wrong.

No value can reassure him because the measurement has been hired to prove treatment success.

A simple repair is scheduled measurement.

If you and a clinician agreed on one rating before and one after, record those and stop.

If you are practicing independently, consider tracking behavior instead: “Did I perform the target ritual?” “Did I return to the activity?”

Behavior is not immune to compulsive checking, but it is usually easier to define.

Exposure that is too vague

“Think about uncertainty” is not a plan.

Neither is “face my fear.”

A useful exposure has a cue and a response-prevention target.

Cue: Read one sentence that raises the relationship doubt.

Response prevention: No feeling checking or mental comparison for fifteen minutes.

Cue: Send a normal work email.

Response prevention: One ordinary proofread only, then no mental reconstruction until the next task is underway.

Specificity helps you discover what failed.

Exposure that is too intense

The opposite problem is overload.

A reader chooses the most frightening scenario because anything less feels like cowardice.

Distress spikes beyond what they can usefully engage with.

They escape, dissociate, ritualize continuously, or decide never to repeat the exercise.

There is no prize for intensity.

Exposure should contact the relevant fear and create a realistic opportunity for response prevention.

A clinician can help adjust intensity, especially when prior attempts have been overwhelming.

The hidden reassurance afterward

Ben completes an exposure, then calls a friend "just to chat."

Within five minutes he mentions the feared topic.

He does not ask the reassurance question directly.

He waits for the friend to say something that answers it.

Reassurance can be elicited indirectly.

The same happens online. A person posts a "general question" in a forum but selects wording likely to invite certainty.

Or they ask a chatbot for "education" and keep rephrasing until the answer feels safe.

The technology is new.

The function is familiar.

When the formulation may be wrong

Not every repetitive thought is OCD.

Not every avoidance pattern calls for ERP.

Depression, generalized anxiety, trauma-related disorders, psychosis, autism-related repetitive behavior, attention problems, medical conditions, substance effects, and other issues can overlap with or resemble parts of OCD.

A self-help book cannot make that differential diagnosis.

If you are applying ERP carefully and the pattern still does not make sense, seek a qualified assessment rather than forcing every symptom into the model.

NIMH notes that OCD diagnosis can be difficult because symptoms can overlap with other mental-health concerns and recommends evaluation by a health professional when symptoms are present (NIMH, 2023).

The troubleshooting audit

Take one stalled exercise and write seven lines:

Target cue.

Target ritual.

Covert substitute.

Post-exposure ritual.

Ordinary safety behavior.

Return action.

One change for the next attempt.

Make only one or two changes.

Do not redesign the entire program after every difficult session.

When to seek specialist review

Professional support is especially useful when:

You are unsure whether the symptoms fit OCD.

Rituals occupy large parts of the day.

Depression or hopelessness is severe.

There is active self-harm or harm risk.

You cannot separate ordinary safety from compulsive safety behavior.

Trauma symptoms are prominent.

Exposure repeatedly becomes overwhelming or destabilizing.

You have tried a reasonable course of ERP and remain significantly impaired.

Look for a clinician who understands OCD and ERP, and tell them explicitly about the covert rituals.

A therapist cannot target a ritual they do not know is happening.

The five most common repairs

When ERP is stuck, five repairs solve more problems than dramatic escalation.

Clarify the compulsion. Replace "stop overthinking" with the exact mental act.

Shorten the plan. Remove unnecessary rules that create performance checking.

Add the substitute. Name the reassurance or feeling check that replaced the original ritual.

Protect the aftermath. Prevent review after the exercise.

Lower the intensity. Choose a repeatable exposure that allows actual response prevention.

These repairs make the method more precise.

They do not guarantee a quick symptom change.

When the book itself becomes reassurance

You may notice yourself returning to the same page.

"Was mental reviewing really listed as a compulsion?"

"Did the author say my exact pattern can happen?"

"Does this example match me closely enough?"

At that point, stop reading.

A book about reassurance can become reassurance.

Use one reading to learn the concept.

Then practice.

If diagnostic doubt is significant, bring it to a professional rather than rereading until you feel certain.

The under-challenge problem

Sometimes a person does exposures that never reach the actual feared meaning.

They choose a trigger that is convenient but not connected to the ritual.

Elena watches romantic films, but her ritual is checking her own feelings.

The film is only useful if it brings the relevant doubt into contact and she prevents the feeling check.

Exposure content should be chosen by function.

Ask, "What cue normally starts the mental ritual?"

That cue is often a better starting point than an impressive-sounding exercise.

The over-control problem

Another stuck pattern is excessive structure.

Every minute is timed.

Every thought is labeled.

Every ritual is recorded.

Every exposure has a script.

Structure can be helpful early.

Too much can create a world in which the reader is constantly managing OCD rather than living.

Gradually allow ordinary situations to become less scripted.

Use the method when needed, then let the task itself take over.

The therapist mismatch question

Not every therapist is trained in ERP, and not every ERP provider is equally comfortable with covert rituals.

If treatment keeps focusing only on visible behavior, ask directly:

"How are we identifying mental rituals?"

"What is the response-prevention target inside the exposure?"

"What should I do with post-exposure rumination?"

"How are we distinguishing ordinary reflection from compulsive review?"

A useful clinician should be able to discuss those questions or refer you appropriately.

You do not need to prove the therapist is wrong.

You need a treatment plan that addresses the behavior you are actually doing.

A two-week troubleshooting pause

If you have been escalating exposures rapidly, consider two weeks devoted to precision.

Do not make tasks harder.

Track the main ritual family.

Practice the same few response-prevention targets.

Look for substitutes and aftermath review.

At the end, decide whether the difficulty needs to change.

Precision before intensity is often a better next move.

The hidden rule audit

Stuck ERP often contains a hidden rule.

"I must feel anxious during exposure."

"I must not reassure myself even once."

"I must catch every ritual immediately."

"I must know whether the thought is an obsession."

"I must do the hardest rung."

Write down the rules you think define a "valid" exposure.

Then sort them.

Some are real treatment principles.

Some are preferences.

Some are OCD rules wearing treatment vocabulary.

If a rule demands perfect internal performance, treat it with suspicion.

A good ERP plan is behaviorally clear but psychologically flexible.

It leaves room for thoughts, feelings, mistakes, and late noticing.

Principles to Remember

When ERP seems stuck, investigate before escalating. Hidden rituals, post-exposure review, recovery checking, vague targets, and excessive intensity can all interfere.

An imperfect exposure does not need to be restarted. Stop the ritual when you notice it and continue.

If the formulation is unclear or symptoms are severe, seek qualified assessment instead of forcing self-help to carry more than it can.

Chapter 15: Daily Life Becomes Practice

Keisha's hardest trigger is not on her hierarchy.

It is the search bar.

She opens her laptop to check a train time and sees the browser history. A phrase from last night's OCD search appears.

The urge is immediate: one more search to make sure the article she read was accurate.

This is not a formal exposure session.

It is Tuesday morning.

That is where most recovery practice eventually has to live.

Ordinary moments have better transfer

Formal exercises are useful because they let you isolate a pattern.

Daily life matters because it is where the pattern has consequences.

Covert rituals attach themselves to gaps in the day: commuting, showering, working, scrolling, waiting for a reply, lying down to sleep, walking between rooms, sitting through a meeting.

You cannot build a separate worksheet for every trigger.

You can carry one question:

What is my mind asking me to settle, and what would I be doing if I did not have to settle it first?

Then cross the moment without performing the ritual as best you can.

Work

Workplace OCD can hide behind conscientiousness.

Read the email again.

Review the meeting.

Check whether the spreadsheet “feels right.”

Rehearse tomorrow's conversation until every possible objection has an answer.

Some checking is part of good work.

The key is the ordinary standard of the role.

If your team proofreads contracts twice, do that.

If your supervisor expects one quality check, do one.

The compulsion is the extra layer added because you need personal certainty beyond the work standard.

Create explicit stopping rules for recurring tasks.

Relationships

Relationships contain endless uncertainty because other people have private minds.

You cannot know every interpretation, every future feeling, or every unspoken reaction.

That makes relationships fertile ground for mental review and silent reassurance.

A useful practice is to separate communication from mind reading.

If there is a real issue, have the conversation.

Ask the ordinary question once.

Listen to the answer.

Then notice when the task shifts to interpreting tone, testing your own feeling, comparing the relationship with others, or replaying the exchange.

Good communication does not require internal certainty afterward.

Online searching

Searching is a visible behavior, but the ritual often continues after the browser closes.

You remember snippets.

You rank sources.

You compare probabilities.

You recall a reassuring sentence.

You decide to search one different phrase because the first result did not answer your exact case.

Use a search rule when the topic is a known compulsion.

Examples:

Follow medical guidance already agreed with a clinician.

Use one trusted source for a practical question.

Do not search the obsessional question during a spike.

If genuinely new symptoms or facts arise, use ordinary care.

The rule should come from your context, not a universal number.

AI and chat reassurance

Generative AI can become a fast reassurance source because it is available at any hour and can answer endless rephrasings.

A person asks, “Does this sound like OCD?”

Then: “But what if I meant the thought?”

Then: “What percentage of people with OCD feel that?”

Then: “Can you be absolutely certain?”

The interface never gets tired.

That makes function especially important.

Use AI for bounded tasks such as organizing notes for a therapy appointment or explaining a general concept.

Do not use it as an oracle for whether your feared possibility is impossible.

If you notice yourself rephrasing the same reassurance question, treat that as the ritual pattern, not as a prompt-engineering problem.

Emerging work has begun examining how generative AI may become involved in reassurance seeking and other compulsive behavior in OCD. A 2026 exploratory qualitative preprint analyzed public OCD discussions about AI and proposed this as a design risk, but this area is new and should not be treated as settled clinical evidence (Barkhuff, 2026).

The behavioral principle does not depend on the technology: repeated certainty seeking remains repeated certainty seeking.

Sleep and empty time

Mental rituals often become louder when external demands decrease.

The temptation is to create a bedtime rule: “I must solve this before I can sleep.”

That is expensive.

Try the opposite rule: bed is not a courtroom.

If a practical task must be remembered, write one neutral note.

Then allow unresolved questions to come to bed without opening the trial.

You may sleep poorly at first.

The goal is not immediate sleep.

It is removing ritual completion as a condition for rest.

Support-person language

A support person can help without becoming a reassurance machine.

Agree on a response outside the spike.

The person might say:

“I hear that the doubt is strong.”

“I am not going to answer the certainty question.”

“Do you want company while you return to what you were doing?”

Support can be warm and specific.

If these lines become a repeated ritual, shorten them.

The relationship is not meant to become an ERP script delivery system.

Three recurring life moments

Pick three predictable moments:

After sending work messages.

After social conversations.

During evening downtime.

At each moment, name one covert ritual you will watch for.

Do not add ten targets.

The point is to move practice out of the exercise container and into life.

A setback in the middle of a normal day

Luis has a difficult week and returns to an old review ritual.

He notices after forty-five minutes.

There is a temptation to declare a relapse, analyze why it happened, and reconstruct every earlier success to determine whether recovery was real.

That would be another review.

Instead, he does something smaller.

He names the ritual.

Stops the current round.

Returns to the task he abandoned.

Schedules a brief review of his plan for the weekend.

The setback becomes information without becoming a trial.

The commute problem

Commuting creates open mental space.

Daniel used to spend twenty minutes replaying drives for possible mistakes.

When he stopped, the first replacement was not peace.

It was the urge to fill the space with another reassurance routine.

He learned to treat the commute as an ordinary activity.

He could listen to music.

He could notice the road.

He could have an intrusive thought.

What he would not do was turn travel time into a mandatory review session.

The lesson transfers to showers, walks, and waiting rooms.

Empty time does not owe OCD an agenda.

Social media and accidental cues

Online life produces a constant stream of words, images, and opinions.

A post may trigger a moral doubt.

A video may trigger a health fear.

A comment may trigger relationship checking.

You do not need to remove every cue.

You also do not need to consume triggering content deliberately all day.

Use ordinary media choices.

When a natural trigger appears, practice response prevention.

If a platform itself has become a compulsive searching environment, create boundaries around the behavior.

The goal is not maximal exposure.

It is freer participation.

Work standards written down

If work checking is a major ritual, write the actual quality standard once.

For example:

"Routine email: one content read, one address check."

"Invoice: follow the department checklist."

"Presentation: one proofread after final edits."

Use the standard consistently.

Do not rewrite it during a spike.

If your role has safety-critical responsibilities, use formal procedures and professional supervision. This book cannot set those standards for you.

Conversations without post-production

Social interactions are not films you can edit afterward.

Grace speaks.

The other person reacts.

The moment moves.

Mental review tries to open a post-production studio.

It changes tone, freezes expressions, and generates alternate cuts.

A simple response-prevention target is: "No editing after the scene."

If concrete feedback arrives, respond to it.

If not, let the conversation remain a completed event with imperfect memory.

Digital support without digital checking

Apps and notes can help treatment.

They can also create endless logs.

Keep digital support sparse.

A short relapse card.

A single list of target rituals.

A weekly review note.

Avoid building a database of every intrusive thought unless a clinician specifically asked for that data.

The objective is to spend less life administering OCD, not more.

The return-to-life list

Write five activities that OCD tends to interrupt.

Examples:

Cooking.

Reading.

Playing with your child.

Writing.

Walking.

Meeting a friend.

When you notice a covert ritual, pick the activity already in front of you rather than inventing a special coping task.

This turns response prevention toward restoration.

You are not simply stopping a behavior.

You are returning time to something else.

The family dinner example

Aisha sits at dinner with relatives and an intrusive religious thought appears.

She feels an urge to repeat a prayer silently.

She begins the first few words before noticing.

She stops.

Then she worries that stopping was disrespectful.

She wants to start again "for the right reason."

That second urge is where covert OCD becomes clever.

The response-prevention action is not to prove disrespect is impossible.

It is to continue dinner while leaving the internal dispute unresolved.

Later, during her ordinary prayer time, Aisha practices her faith according to her normal routine.

Treatment does not require abandoning what matters.

It requires separating ordinary practice from emergency repetition demanded by a spike.

In a Nutshell

Daily life is where covert response prevention becomes flexible. Work, relationships, searching, AI tools, and quiet time all create ordinary uncertainty.

Use normal standards for real tasks. Communicate when communication is needed. Then stop the extra layer of certainty work.

When a setback appears, respond to the current ritual. You do not need to reconstruct your entire recovery to decide what to do next.

Chapter 16: Keep Recovery Flexible

Marcus notices the new theme before he notices the old process.

For months his OCD centered on health.

Now the trigger is morality.

He remembers a small lie from years ago and feels the familiar demand to reconstruct what happened, decide how much harm it caused, and determine what the memory says about his character.

At first he thinks, *This is different. My health work does not apply.*

Then he sees the structure.

Signal.

Urge.

Review.

Reassurance.

The subject changed.

The Answering Line did not.

Theme migration

OCD content can change over time. NIMH notes that a person's obsessions and compulsions can change (NIMH, 2023).

That is one reason this book has focused on function rather than building a separate treatment manual for every theme.

If you learn only “how to respond to health thoughts,” a moral thought can feel like a new disorder.

If you learn “how I use mental review to obtain certainty,” the new content may be easier to recognize.

The feared story can change.

The ritual family often remains familiar.

Lapse is not a verdict

A lapse is a return to a ritual.

It does not answer whether treatment worked.

It does not prove you have lost all progress.

It is a behavior that happened.

The next useful question is behavioral too:

"What is the next ritual I can decline?"

If you spend hours proving that the lapse "does not count," you have turned recovery into reassurance.

If you spend hours condemning yourself for the lapse, you may have turned it into moral rumination.

Repair is smaller.

Notice.

Stop.

Return.

Review the plan later at a scheduled time.

Early signals

Your warning signs may be subtle.

You start rereading old notes about OCD.

You ask friends "hypothetical" questions.

You spend longer deciding whether a thought is obsession or compulsion.

You check anxiety after exposures.

You postpone ordinary tasks until a doubt feels settled.

You use treatment phrases more often but act less.

Write four personal signs.

Keep them behavioral when possible.

"Feeling anxious" is too broad.

"Reading the same reassurance article three times" is specific.

Scheduled review

Some reflection on treatment is useful.

Constant reflection is not.

Choose a regular review window, perhaps weekly, if that fits your situation.

Ask:

What ritual family showed up most?

Where did I notice the Answering Line sooner?

Where did I substitute one certainty behavior for another?

What ordinary activity did I reclaim?

What one target will I practice next?

Then end the review.

Do not turn the weekly check into a verdict about your identity, prognosis, or perfect adherence.

Progress by behavior

Symptom intensity can fluctuate.

Thought frequency can fluctuate.

Anxiety can fluctuate.

Progress can still be measured by what you do.

Did you shorten a review?

Did you ask one fewer reassurance question?

Did you send the email after the ordinary check?

Did you return to the conversation while uncertainty remained?

Did you seek professional help when self-directed work reached its limit?

Those are meaningful changes because they concern participation and choice.

Treatment research evaluates symptoms in broader ways than this simple scorecard, but for everyday self-monitoring, behavior-based questions reduce the temptation to use a feeling as the verdict.

When to return to professional care

Self-help should have an exit ramp.

Return to qualified care when symptoms are expanding, functioning is deteriorating, depression is worsening, risk is present, rituals consume large portions of the day, or you cannot safely design response prevention.

You may also need a clinician simply because a covert ritual is hard to see from inside.

That is not a failure of the method.

It is an appropriate use of another person's trained perspective.

The relapse card

Write a short card, physical or digital.

My common signals: four specific behaviors.

My common covert rituals: two or three.

My first response: one non-engagement action.

My ordinary activity to return to: one example.

My support plan: who to contact if symptoms are significantly interfering.

My safety line: when I will seek urgent help rather than treating the situation as an ERP exercise.

Keep it brief enough to read without analyzing.

A final example

Priya, months after the work-email episode in Chapter 1, receives a text from a family member that ends abruptly.

Her old pattern would be to reconstruct the previous conversation and decide whether she had caused offense.

The urge is strong.

She catches it after two minutes, not immediately.

She notices she is reviewing tone.

She stops mid-replay.

She sends no reassurance-seeking text.

She continues making lunch.

Later the family member calls and explains that the phone battery died.

Priya could use that explanation as proof that response prevention is safe.

She does something more useful.

She notices that the outcome is incidental.

The practice was continuing her day before she had the explanation.

Your pattern fingerprint

By the end of this book, you may know your content well.

More useful is knowing your **pattern fingerprint**.

Perhaps your sequence is:

Trigger.

Moral doubt.

Memory review.

Feeling check.

Silent reassurance.

Search.

Or:

Body sensation.

Catastrophic possibility.

Internal comparison.

Doctor-quote reassurance.

Recovery check.

Write the sequence in verbs.

Review.

Compare.

Check.

Reassure.

Search.

Repeat.

Verbs travel across themes better than nouns.

What to do when a new theme feels convincing

A new theme usually feels more convincing than an old one.

That is why it is new.

The mind says, "The old ones were OCD. This one is real."

Do not try to prove that the new theme is also OCD.

That proof can become reassurance.

Instead, inspect the behavior.

Are you performing the same mental review?

Are you checking the same internal state?

Are you asking for the same certainty?

If yes, use the same response-prevention principle while leaving diagnosis questions to proper clinical assessment when needed.

Scheduled maintenance

Maintenance does not require daily obsession management.

A brief weekly or monthly check may be enough when things are stable.

Ask what activities have expanded.

Ask which rituals are quietly returning.

Choose one practice.

Then stop reviewing.

Maintenance should be lighter than acute treatment.

If it becomes a major time commitment, ask whether recovery checking has taken over.

Respond early, not perfectly

Early response does not mean catching the first thought.

It means acting before the pattern has grown into a full system again.

If you notice three nights of mental review, tighten the response-prevention plan.

If reassurance seeking is increasing, talk with your support person.

If functioning is slipping, contact a clinician sooner rather than waiting for a crisis.

The best relapse plan is not “never lapse.”

It is “recognize the pattern and respond while options are still broad.”

Recovery and uncertainty about recovery

There is one final obsessional question:

“Will I be okay?”

No book can answer it with certainty.

No treatment can promise a symptom-free future.

You can build skills.

You can seek evidence-based care.

You can practice response prevention.

You can return to ordinary life repeatedly.

Then uncertainty remains.

That is not a defect in the plan.

It is the same human condition the plan has been teaching you to live inside.

A letter to your future self

Write six sentences.

Name your most common ritual family.

Name the Answering Line cue you tend to miss.

Name the ordinary action that helps you return.

Name one support person or professional route.

Name the safety condition that requires urgent help.

End with: "I do not need to prove that recovery is still real before I use the next skill."

Keep the letter.

Do not reread it for reassurance.

Use it when the plan has genuinely become hard to remember.

When improvement feels suspicious

Improvement can itself trigger OCD.

"If the thought bothers me less, maybe that proves I secretly agree with it."

"If I need less reassurance, maybe I was never responsible."

"If I can leave a memory alone, maybe I do not care what happened."

The mind converts reduced distress into new evidence.

This is a familiar feeling-check structure.

Do not restore anxiety to prove morality.

Do not reopen a ritual to prove the fear is still unwanted.

Let improvement be ambiguous too.

Your job is behavior.

If real responsibility appears, address it.

Otherwise, keep using the same skills without demanding that recovery feel morally safe.

Principles to Remember

Themes can change while the ritual function stays recognizable. Follow the process rather than rebuilding treatment around every new subject.

A lapse is behavior, not a verdict. Respond to the next ritual rather than reviewing the entire past.

Use scheduled, behavior-based review. Keep a short relapse card and a clear line for returning to professional care.

Conclusion: The Mind Can Stay Unanswered

The hardest part of covert OCD is often not the first thought.

It is everything recruited after it.

The replay.

The internal debate.

The remembered fact.

The check for guilt, attraction, certainty, disgust, sincerity, or "rightness."

The quiet sentence designed to make the question go away.

Those acts can happen so quickly and privately that they feel inseparable from consciousness itself.

They are not.

The Answering Line gives you a practical place to look.

What showed up?

What did you add?

What was the added mental work trying to settle?

What ordinary action was waiting while you tried to settle it?

That sequence will not always be clear. Sometimes you will catch the ritual after forty minutes. Sometimes a phrase you learned for response prevention will itself become reassurance. Sometimes the theme will change and the old process will look new.

The standard is not perfect detection.

It is repeated opportunity.

ERP has two parts for a reason. Exposure contacts the feared or uncertain cue. Response prevention changes what you do next. When the compulsion is mental, the second half still matters.

You can allow a thought without answering it.

You can remember something without reconstructing it.

You can feel something without measuring it.

You can receive information without using it as a repeated guarantee.

You can make an ordinary decision without converting it into proof of who you are.

You can return to a task before your mind has issued a final verdict.

None of those choices guarantees a particular feeling.

That is part of the work.

A useful recovery question is therefore not, "Am I certain now?"

It is, "What would I do next if I did not need this question settled first?"

Then do that thing at an ordinary standard.

Send the email.

Finish lunch.

Stay in the conversation.

Go to bed.

Follow the medical plan already agreed with your clinician.

Ask for professional help when the problem is larger than self-help can safely hold.

The mind may continue producing questions.

It does not have to receive an answer every time.

Appendix A: The Covert Ritual Field Guide

This field guide is a condensed way to classify patterns you have already learned. Use it to orient yourself, not to prove that every mental event fits a category.

Rumination

What it looks like: Repeatedly analyzing a question, generating explanations, comparing possibilities, or trying to reason your way to certainty.

Common private language: "I need to understand why." "One more angle." "If I think carefully enough, this will make sense."

The function question: "What real decision will this thinking allow me to make?"

Response-prevention direction: Make the ordinary decision if one exists, then stop the extra trial. Let the unanswered part remain unanswered.

Common substitute: Searching online for information that allows the rumination to continue with new material.

Mental reviewing

What it looks like: Replaying a conversation, drive, decision, memory, or bodily event to establish what happened or what it meant.

Common private language: "Let me go through it one more time." "I almost remember." "If I can get the sequence right, I will know."

The function question: "Is there new external information that makes another review necessary?"

Response-prevention direction: Follow ordinary reporting or repair procedures if facts require them. Otherwise leave the memory incomplete.

Common substitute: Asking another person to reconstruct the event for you.

Silent reassurance

What it looks like: Supplying yourself with facts, statistics, remembered professional statements, diagnostic labels, or moral arguments.

Common private language: "I have never done that before." "My doctor said…" "This fits OCD." "A good person would not…"

The function question: "Am I using information for an action, or repeating it because certainty has faded?"

Response-prevention direction: Decline the next internal verdict and return to behavior.

Common substitute: Asking a person, search engine, forum, or chatbot the same question in new wording.

Feeling checks

What it looks like: Scanning attraction, guilt, fear, disgust, sincerity, anxiety, certainty, or "rightness."

Common private language: "How do I feel right now?" "Is that enough?" "Why did the feeling change?"

The function question: "What verdict am I asking this feeling to provide?"

Response-prevention direction: Allow the state to be noticed without scoring or interpreting it.

Common substitute: Repeating the trigger to see whether the feeling changes.

Neutralizing

What it looks like: Replacing, canceling, correcting, balancing, counting, repeating, or mentally undoing unwanted content.

Common private language: "I need to get the bad thought out." "I have to say it correctly." "I need the good image after the bad one."

The function question: "Would I still do this if it did not reduce the threat or make the thought feel corrected?"

Response-prevention direction: Let the unwanted content remain uncorrected while preserving ordinary faith, values, and safety.

Common substitute: Using a therapeutic phrase as the new canceling phrase.

Recovery checking

What it looks like: Repeatedly measuring whether ERP is working, whether anxiety is right, whether acceptance feels genuine, or whether a thought was classified correctly.

Common private language: "Did that count?" "Was I secretly reassuring?" "Am I improving?"

The function question: "Is this measurement part of a scheduled treatment plan, or am I using it to obtain certainty now?"

Response-prevention direction: Use scheduled, behavior-based review and let the rest remain unclear.

Common substitute: Reading treatment material repeatedly to prove the method applies.

The field-guide rule

Do not use this guide more often than needed.

If you find yourself opening it every time a thought appears, stop.

You already know the central question:

What showed up, what did I add, and what was the added mental work trying to settle?

That question is enough for most moments.

Appendix B: Exposure Design Examples

The examples below are educational models, not personalized treatment prescriptions. Keep ordinary safety, use low-to-moderate starting points for self-directed practice, and involve a qualified OCD clinician when symptoms are severe, risks are unclear, or prior exposure attempts have been destabilizing.

Harm doubt with silent reassurance

Pattern: An unwanted harm image appears. The person then lists reasons they are not dangerous.

Possible cue: Read a neutral phrase such as "I cannot get complete certainty about what thoughts mean."

Response prevention: Do not list character evidence, check disgust, or ask another person for reassurance.

Return action: Continue the ordinary activity already underway.

Safety boundary: Do not use actual dangerous behavior, unsafe weapons handling, reckless driving, or other genuine hazards as exposure.

Moral memory with reviewing

Pattern: A vague memory triggers repeated reconstruction of whether the person acted wrongly.

Possible cue: Write, "There may be details I do not remember."

Response prevention: Do not reconstruct sequence, motive, tone, or missing details unless genuinely new external information creates a practical responsibility.

Return action: Resume work, household tasks, conversation, or another planned activity.

Safety boundary: If there is concrete evidence of real harm or a legal responsibility, use appropriate professional or practical procedures. ERP is not a reason to ignore facts.

Relationship doubt with feeling checks

Pattern: A relationship thought leads to repeated monitoring of love, attraction, warmth, or certainty.

Possible cue: Spend ordinary time with the partner while allowing relationship uncertainty to be present.

Response prevention: Do not scan attraction, compare feelings with previous days, or test reactions to photos or imagined breakups.

Return action: Participate in the actual conversation or activity.

Safety boundary: ERP should not be used to dismiss abuse, coercion, or concrete safety concerns.

Health doubt with internal reassurance

Pattern: A familiar sensation triggers memory of a doctor's reassuring sentence and repeated internal comparison.

Possible cue: Allow the ordinary sensation to be present without extra scanning.

Response prevention: Follow the medical plan already given. Do not add repeated body checks, remembered reassurance, or repeated searching.

Return action: Continue the day's task.

Safety boundary: New or worsening symptoms that meet medical guidance should receive ordinary medical attention. A book cannot assess a symptom.

Social doubt with post-event review

Pattern: After a conversation, the person replays words and expressions to decide whether they were disliked or offensive.

Possible cue: Attend a normal social interaction.

Response prevention: No replay after the ordinary interaction. Respond to concrete feedback if it appears.

Return action: Move to the next activity.

Safety boundary: Genuine interpersonal repair remains available. Response prevention targets speculation, not accountability.

Religious doubt with neutralizing

Pattern: An intrusive thought triggers repeated prayer, confession, or mental correction beyond ordinary religious practice.

Possible cue: Allow the intrusive thought to occur during ordinary life.

Response prevention: Follow the pre-agreed ordinary religious practice without extra repetition demanded by the spike.

Return action: Continue the current task or planned observance.

Safety boundary: When religious duty is genuinely unclear, seek guidance from an informed religious leader who understands OCD and, when possible, an OCD-trained clinician.

Memory doubt after driving

Pattern: The driver replays the road to prove no accident occurred.

Possible cue: Complete an ordinary drive using all normal driving laws and safety practices.

Response prevention: Do not mentally reconstruct the route after arrival unless a real external event requires it.

Return action: Enter the destination and begin the next task.

Safety boundary: Never reduce actual driving attention or ignore evidence of an incident. Driving itself must remain safe.

"Just right" mental repetition

Pattern: A word, phrase, or image is repeated until it feels complete.

Possible cue: Say or read the relevant ordinary phrase once.

Response prevention: Do not repeat to obtain the internal click.

Return action: Continue the sentence, task, prayer, or conversation.

Safety boundary: Do not interfere with safety-critical communication or professional procedures.

Diagnostic doubt

Pattern: The person repeatedly checks whether the thought "really is OCD."

Possible cue: Notice the diagnostic question.

Response prevention: Do not repeat symptom tests, reread the same diagnostic page, or seek repeated certainty from others.

Return action: Follow the treatment plan already established or schedule one appropriate clinical assessment if diagnosis is genuinely unresolved.

Safety boundary: Self-help cannot diagnose. New symptoms or significant diagnostic uncertainty deserve qualified evaluation.

The design checklist in prose

Before each exposure, say what you are contacting.

Name the main covert ritual.

Name one or two likely substitutes.

State the ordinary safety behavior that remains.

Choose the return action.

Choose how the exercise ends.

Choose the post-exposure response-prevention window.

That is enough.

Do not turn exposure design into another perfection task.

Appendix C: Working With an OCD Clinician

A focused book can help you describe a problem that is difficult to describe.

It cannot replace a clinician's ability to assess diagnosis, risk, comorbidity, medical context, and treatment fit.

If you seek professional help, bring the covert rituals into the room explicitly.

What to say at the first appointment

You do not need a polished explanation.

Try:

"My main rituals are mental. I replay memories, reassure myself silently, and check how I feel."

"I have done exposure before, but I think I continued ritualizing in my head."

"I need help distinguishing obsessional material from the mental response."

"I would like the response-prevention target to include covert rituals."

Concrete verbs are useful.

Review.

Compare.

Check.

Reassure.

Neutralize.

Repeat.

Search.

A clinician can ask better questions when the behavior is named.

Questions about treatment fit

You can ask:

"How do you identify mental compulsions in ERP?"

"How do you handle post-exposure rumination?"

"How do you distinguish non-engagement from suppression?"

"How do you decide when imaginal exposure is appropriate?"

"How do you keep response prevention from removing ordinary safety?"

"How do you measure progress without turning measurement into ritual?"

The goal is not to interrogate the clinician.

It is to learn how the treatment addresses the problem you actually have.

Bring examples, not a perfect history

One or two recent loops may be more useful than a complete autobiography.

Write the trigger.

Write the obsessional question.

Write the visible behavior.

Write the mental behavior.

Write what the mental behavior was trying to obtain.

If you are uncertain about classification, say so.

That uncertainty is clinically useful information.

If you have already tried ERP

Do not summarize the entire experience as "ERP failed."

Describe what happened.

Which exposures did you do?

Which visible rituals did you prevent?

Which mental rituals continued?

What did you do after exposures?

How often did you seek reassurance?

Did you track anxiety repeatedly?

Did the exposure target the actual feared meaning?

Those details can reveal whether the issue was treatment fit, delivery, adherence, hidden rituals, comorbidity, or something else.

A book cannot determine which explanation applies.

A clinician can investigate.

Medication questions

Medication can be part of OCD treatment. NIMH notes that OCD treatment may involve psychotherapy, medication, or both (NIMH, 2023).

Do not change medication because of exposure progress, a passage in this book, or an online comment.

Discuss dose, side effects, starting, stopping, and interactions with the prescribing professional.

If you notice yourself repeatedly checking whether medication is "working" from hour to hour, bring that behavior to treatment too.

When another condition may be involved

Tell the clinician about depression, trauma history, panic, substance use, eating concerns, psychotic symptoms, attention problems, autism, medical conditions, sleep problems, or other relevant issues.

That does not mean any of those explains the OCD.

It means good treatment planning looks at the whole picture.

Self-help narrows attention by design.

Clinical assessment should not.

Appendix D: A Guide for Support People

If someone you care about has covert OCD, you may see less of the ritual than they do.

That can make it tempting to judge progress by whether they look calm.

Do not.

A person can be quiet while reviewing intensely.

They can also look distressed while successfully resisting a ritual.

Behavior and distress are not the same thing.

What reassurance sounds like

Reassurance may be direct:

“Do you think I did something wrong?”

“Are you sure I am safe?”

“Does this sound like OCD?”

It may be indirect:

“Hypothetically, what would you think if someone…”

“Would a bad person worry this much?”

“Can I tell you the story one more time?”

The person may not be manipulating you.

They may be trying to reduce uncertainty in the only way that feels available.

Compassion and participation are different.

You can care without answering the same certainty question repeatedly.

Agree on language outside the spike

Do not invent a boundary during the most distressed moment if you can plan earlier.

Ask the person and, if applicable, their clinician what response is useful.

A possible agreement:

“I will listen once to practical information.”

“I will not repeatedly decide whether the feared event is impossible.”

“I can remind you of the response-prevention plan once.”

“I can stay nearby while you return to the activity.”

“I will respond normally to genuinely new information.”

The exact plan should fit the relationship.

Avoid becoming a therapist

A partner, friend, or parent is not responsible for delivering ERP perfectly.

Do not monitor every sentence.

Do not accuse the person of ritualizing.

Do not turn ordinary conversation into a clinical session.

If you notice a repeated reassurance loop, use the agreed response.

Then return to being a partner, friend, or family member.

Warmth without certainty

You can say:

"I know this is hard."

"I am not going to answer the certainty question."

"I can sit with you while you finish dinner."

"Do you want to go back to what we were doing?"

These responses acknowledge the person without certifying the feared content.

If even these sentences become requested ritualistically, shorten them.

When safety changes the plan

Do not withhold help when there is a genuine emergency.

If the person expresses intent or a plan to harm themselves or someone else, cannot stay safe, is severely medically unwell, or is otherwise in immediate danger, seek appropriate emergency help.

A reassurance-reduction plan is not an emergency protocol.

Safety takes priority.

Appendix E: Safety Boundaries for Self Directed ERP

ERP is exposure to feared or uncertain cues with prevention of compulsive responses.

It is not a license to create real danger.

The distinction needs to be explicit in self-help because OCD often targets the same domains in which real risks can exist.

Medical uncertainty

Follow ordinary medical guidance.

Do not ignore symptoms that a clinician has told you to report.

Do not stop medication.

Do not skip medically indicated tests as an "exposure."

If a behavior such as repeated body checking or repeated appointments is part of health OCD, work with a clinician to decide what ordinary medical care looks like.

The exposure is to the uncertainty left after appropriate care.

Driving and public safety

Follow traffic laws.

Maintain attention to driving.

Respond to real evidence of a collision or hazard.

Do not deliberately drive unsafely.

For hit-and-run obsessions, the response-prevention target may be repeated route review, mirror checking beyond ordinary driving, retracing, or mental reconstruction after a normal drive. The safety behavior of driving responsibly stays.

Harm and self-harm themes

Intrusive harm thoughts can be part of OCD, and NIMH includes unwanted aggressive thoughts among common obsession examples (NIMH, 2023).

But a book cannot determine whether a specific thought is an obsession or an intention.

If you have a plan, intent, access to means you may use, or concern that you cannot remain safe, seek immediate local crisis or emergency support.

Self-directed ERP should not involve actual dangerous behavior.

Work and legal responsibilities

Do not use response prevention to ignore a legal, regulatory, fiduciary, or safety-critical duty.

If your job requires a checklist, complete it.

If a law requires reporting, follow it.

If uncertainty concerns a serious legal obligation, seek qualified legal or professional advice rather than treating the question as OCD by default.

The compulsion is the extra certainty behavior beyond the real standard.

Relationships and abuse

ERP is not a method for tolerating abuse.

Concrete evidence of violence, coercion, stalking, exploitation, or danger requires safety planning and appropriate support.

Relationship OCD can involve doubts in otherwise ordinary relationships, but a self-help framework should never be used to erase real evidence.

Religion and ethics

Do not ask this book to decide doctrine.

Work with informed religious leadership and an OCD clinician when compulsions and sincere practice are difficult to separate.

The same applies to complex ethical duties.

ERP should reduce compulsive certainty seeking without demanding abandonment of actual values.

When to stop self-directed escalation

Stop increasing exposure intensity and seek professional help when:

You cannot tell whether the task is safe.

Distress becomes unmanageable.

You are dissociating or losing functional control.

Depression or hopelessness is worsening.

You have active self-harm or harm risk.

You suspect psychosis or another condition that changes how exposure should be used.

You are spending more time designing ERP than living.

You keep creating increasingly extreme exercises to prove commitment.

Self-directed work is one level of support.

Using more support when needed is an ordinary treatment decision.

Appendix F: A Compact Practice Library

This final section gathers short practices from the book so you can use them without rereading whole chapters.

Do not use the library as reassurance.

Choose one practice.

Use it.

Close the book.

The four-line loop

Trigger.

What showed up.

What I added mentally.

What the added act was trying to give me.

This is the simplest observation tool.

The function question

"What am I trying to know, feel, prevent, prove, cancel, or settle?"

Ask once.

Do not analyze the answer.

The decision test

"What real-world decision will this thinking allow me to make?"

If there is one, make it at an ordinary standard.

If there is not, consider response prevention.

The new-information test

"Has genuinely new external information appeared?"

If yes, respond appropriately.

If no, do not reopen the internal case only because confidence fell.

The gray-zone rule

If you cannot quickly classify a mental event as obsession or compulsion, do not solve the classification.

Return to the next useful action.

Notice, decline, return

Notice the obsessional question.

Decline the certainty work.

Return to one concrete action.

Repeat when needed.

The post-exposure window

Before exposure, decide how long you will prevent delayed review, reassurance, checking, or research afterward.

During the window, do ordinary activities.

Do not grade the exposure.

The substitute question

"If I could not use my usual ritual, what would I do instead to get the same certainty?"

Name one or two likely substitutes before practice.

The ordinary-safety rule

Keep the legal, ethical, medical, and practical precautions that make sense without OCD's demand for extra certainty.

When safety is unclear, ask a qualified professional.

The behavior score

Instead of "How anxious am I?"

Try:

"Did I perform the named ritual?"

"Did I notice and stop a substitute?"

"Did I return to the activity?"

Use scheduled review only.

The ordinary-action question

"What would I do next if I did not need this question settled first?"

Then begin that action.

The closing rule

A practice ends when the plan says it ends, not when you feel certain, calm, correct, sincere, or finished.

That rule may be the most useful response prevention of all.

Appendix G: Theme Translation: Seven Full Walkthroughs

The content of an obsession can change dramatically while the ritual structure stays familiar. One reader worries about a relationship. Another worries about harm. Another is stuck on a memory that cannot be reconstructed with certainty. If the work stays at the level of theme, each new topic can feel like a new problem that requires a new answer. The purpose of these walkthroughs is different. Each example follows the same sequence: notice what arrived, identify what the mind starts doing in response, find the Answering Line, choose response prevention, and return to ordinary action.

These examples are educational, not diagnostic templates. Real situations can include practical duties, genuine danger, trauma, medical concerns, legal issues, or other problems that deserve direct attention. The point is to see how the method transfers when OCD is already the working formulation.

Walkthrough 1: Relationship doubt

Maya is making coffee when the thought appears: "What if I do not love my partner enough?" The first sentence arrives quickly. She did not schedule it. Within seconds, however, she begins scanning the previous evening. Was she excited enough when her partner came home? Did she laugh naturally? Did the hug feel warm? She then compares the relationship with an earlier one and silently repeats three reasons the current relationship is good.

The obsession is not every thought about the relationship. The useful distinction is functional. The initial doubt is the signal. The replay, comparison, feeling check, and internal case for the relationship are responses recruited to settle the doubt. They are on the ritual side of the Answering Line.

Maya's response-prevention target is therefore not “never think about my relationship.” It is narrower: when the obsessional question appears, do not run an internal test of whether love feels sufficient. She can notice the question and continue making coffee. If a genuine relationship decision requires thought later, she can choose a time, define the practical question, and stop when the decision task is complete. She does not have to reach a special internal feeling first.

An exposure might be ordinary rather than dramatic. Maya could read a neutral sentence such as, “I cannot obtain perfect certainty about how I will feel in this relationship in the future,” then prepare breakfast without checking for reassurance. The learning target is not that the relationship is safe or unsafe. It is that a meaningful relationship can continue without an internal verdict every time doubt appears.

A common substitute is behavioral testing. Maya may stop mental review but begin watching her partner's face, checking how much she misses them during the day, or searching online for signs of a “wrong relationship.” The form has changed, but the function has not. Her plan therefore includes the substitute: no deliberate tests of feeling, no repeated comparison with past relationships, and no reassurance search after the exposure.

The return matters. She chooses a normal next action, such as packing lunch or answering a work message. If doubt stays present, it can come along. Response prevention is measured by what she stops doing for certainty, not by whether affection or calm appears on command.

Walkthrough 2: Harm and responsibility

Marcus is driving home when he feels a small bump in the road. A thought appears: “What if that was a person?” He checks the mirror once as part of ordinary driving. Nothing unusual is visible. Ten seconds later, his mind begins reconstructing the sound, the position of parked cars, the last pedestrian he saw, and whether the steering wheel moved. He feels an urge to turn around.

In this example, ordinary safety and compulsion must be separated before the anxiety spike becomes the rule maker. A driver has normal responsibilities after an actual collision, a witnessed hazard, or concrete evidence of an accident. Those responsibilities do not require a person to ignore genuine danger. The OCD problem begins when ordinary information has been exhausted and the mind demands repeated proof against a hypothetical possibility.

For Marcus, the Answering Line appears after the ordinary check. The extended reconstruction, repeated mirror checking, route retracing, and search for the "right" memory feeling are attempts to eliminate residual uncertainty. His response-prevention plan is based on a preselected ordinary-driving standard rather than a confidence percentage. When that standard is met, he continues the trip.

The exposure is built into the moment: the unresolved possibility remains available to awareness while he drives on. He does not need to repeat a frightening sentence until numbness appears. He also does not need to reassure himself that "it was definitely a pothole." Both could become rituals. His task is behavioral: follow the ordinary safety rule, decline extra checking, and continue to the next destination.

Later, the obsession may return as mental review: "But what exactly did that sound like?" This is the delayed version of the same ritual. Marcus labels the function rather than reopening the case. He can say, if useful, "That is a request for another check," and resume what he was doing.

If there is genuine evidence of harm, a real-world response comes first. The method is not a license to dismiss facts. It is a way to stop hypothetical doubt from creating an unlimited safety standard.

Walkthrough 3: Moral scrupulosity

Aisha remembers a sharp comment she made in a meeting. She has already decided that the tone was unnecessary and sent a brief apology to the colleague involved. The next morning, the memory returns with a new question: “What if the apology itself was manipulative?” She rereads the message in memory, evaluates every word, checks whether she felt sincere enough while typing, and imagines how an ideally moral person would have handled the situation.

This case shows why genuine repair and compulsion can sit next to each other. The apology may be an ordinary value-based action. The hours of post-repair analysis do not become useful merely because the topic is ethics. The question is whether new information is being used to guide a concrete action or whether the mind is trying to obtain moral certainty.

Aisha marks the Answering Line at the point where the practical repair is complete. She does not need to prove that she is a good person before returning to work. Her response prevention includes no repeated rereading of the message, no internal character trial, and no new confession to coworkers solely to make guilt disappear.

An exposure might be the ordinary fact that moral action does not provide perfect knowledge of character. Aisha can allow the sentence, “I may never know exactly how that moment reflects on me,” and then act according to her values now. She can be courteous in the next meeting because courtesy matters, not because the behavior proves innocence.

The substitute ritual to watch is values-as-reassurance. A person can turn “I care about being kind” into evidence that the feared meaning is impossible. That is different from using values to choose behavior. Values answer, "What do I want to do next?" They do not have to answer, "What does this prove about who I am?"

When the memory returns later, Aisha does not need to suppress it. She lets it be present without restarting the trial. The practice is not moral indifference. It is refusing to make certainty the price of acting responsibly.

Walkthrough 4: Memory and false-memory doubt

Luis wakes with a fragment of memory from a party months earlier. He cannot tell whether one part actually happened or whether he imagined it later. The question feels urgent because the feared possibility would matter to him. He begins rebuilding the night in sequence: who arrived first, where he was standing, what he drank, what a friend said, what time he left. Each pass produces a slightly different version.

The mind interprets variation as evidence that more reconstruction is required. That is the trap. Memory review can feel investigative even when it is no longer producing new external information. The stopping rule becomes confidence, and confidence can remain unstable under repeated checking.

Luis uses the new-evidence test. Has a new message, record, witness statement, or other ordinary source of information appeared? If not, another internal replay is not new evidence. It is the same material being queried again. The Answering Line is crossed when remembering turns into repeated certainty work.

Response prevention means allowing an incomplete record to remain incomplete. Luis does not force a conclusion that nothing happened. He also does not manufacture a conclusion that something did. He stops rebuilding the scene once the practical information available to him has been considered by an ordinary standard.

For exposure, he may write one short statement: “My memory of that night is incomplete, and I cannot make it perfect by replaying it.” He reads it once or at a planned frequency and then returns to the present task. The purpose is not to make the sentence feel acceptable. It is to practice not converting uncertainty into another reconstruction.

If new factual information appears later, he can respond to it. Response prevention does not require stubbornly ignoring evidence. It prevents the absence of certainty from being treated as evidence that endless review is necessary.

Walkthrough 5: Identity and attraction checking

Sofia notices an image of someone on a television program and immediately asks herself what her reaction means about her identity. Attention narrows to her body. She checks for warmth, tension, interest, aversion, or a sense of recognition. When the sensations are ambiguous, she repeats the image mentally. Then she compares the response with memories of other people.

The visible topic is identity. The covert ritual is measurement. Sofia is trying to turn variable internal states into a definitive test. The first task is not to decide what every sensation means. It is to notice when deliberate checking begins.

Her Answering Line sits between an experience and the test of that experience. Attraction, discomfort, curiosity, numbness, and uncertainty can occur without requiring immediate analysis. The ritual begins when she repeatedly evokes, compares, or scores those reactions in order to reach certainty.

Response prevention removes the test. Sofia allows the original image or thought to remain in memory without replaying it to gather better data. She does not compare one person with another. She does not ask whether the absence of a sensation is meaningful. She returns attention to the program as a program.

This does not mean identity questions can never be explored. Ordinary self-reflection can be chosen rather than triggered, can consider a broad pattern of life rather than a single anxiety-driven test, and can stop without perfect certainty. If reflection repeatedly becomes a demand for immediate proof, that is useful information about function.

A possible exposure is to let an ambiguous reaction stay ambiguous for the rest of the evening. No conclusion is required. The practical outcome is not a particular identity label. It is greater freedom from compulsive testing as the method of finding one.

Walkthrough 6: Health-related rumination

Daniel notices a familiar headache after a long day. He has a medical plan for when headaches require care and when routine self-care is appropriate. Tonight none of the agreed warning signs are present. Even so, he begins mentally listing serious causes, checking whether the pain feels "different," replaying what he ate, and asking himself whether he has overlooked a symptom.

Health themes require a careful boundary because real bodies sometimes need real medical attention. ERP should not replace appropriate evaluation, emergency care, screening, or advice from a qualified clinician. That is why Daniel's ordinary-safety rule is defined outside the spike and follows the plan he has already made with appropriate professionals.

Once the ordinary rule is met, repeated internal diagnosis becomes the target. The Answering Line is crossed when Daniel moves from noticing a symptom and following his plan to trying to eliminate every residual possibility through repeated analysis. The ritual may include body checking, online searching, memory review, or silently repeating previous medical reassurance.

His response prevention is not "ignore symptoms." It is "follow the ordinary care rule once, then do not add anxiety-driven certainty procedures." If a genuinely new sign appears, the rule can be applied again. If nothing new appears, a rise in fear alone does not automatically create a new medical task.

Exposure may simply be continuing the evening while the unresolved thought remains: "I cannot obtain perfect health certainty tonight." Daniel prepares dinner and leaves the question unanswered. He does not use the sentence to force calm.

The distinction between care and compulsion is often clearest before distress rises. Written medical guidance, when appropriate, can define the safety boundary. ERP then begins on the other side of that boundary.

Walkthrough 7: Therapy and recovery checking

Priya has been practicing ERP for several weeks. One morning she notices that an intrusive thought feels less intense. Instead of enjoying the extra room in her day, she begins asking, "Is this real improvement? What if I am suppressing? Did I do yesterday's exposure correctly?" She reviews the previous session, rates her anxiety, and compares today's thought frequency with last Tuesday.

Recovery itself has become the obsessional topic. This is easy to miss because the questions sound responsible. The function reveals the problem. Priya is not collecting information for a scheduled treatment decision. She is repeatedly checking whether recovery is safe, valid, and correctly performed.

Her Answering Line is crossed when useful review becomes immediate reassurance seeking about the process. A planned weekly check-in with a clinician can be ordinary. Ten unscheduled internal audits before lunch are not made necessary by the word "therapy."

Response prevention means returning to behavioral measures. Did Priya approach the planned trigger? Did she reduce the target ritual? Did she return to ordinary activity? Those questions can be reviewed at the planned time. In the moment, she does not need to determine whether she feels recovered enough.

An exposure can be subtle: deliberately leave one treatment question unanswered until the next scheduled review. She might notice, “Maybe I did that exposure imperfectly,” and continue with her morning. The aim is not carelessness. It is flexibility.

A substitute ritual is rereading treatment books, saved notes, or therapist messages for certainty. Educational material is useful when it teaches a skill or supports a planned decision. It becomes part of the loop when the same passage is consulted again and again to obtain a verdict.

The final transfer is important. ERP is not only exposure to feared life content. Sometimes it includes uncertainty about ERP itself. Recovery becomes more flexible when the method does not require proof of perfect recovery.

What transfers across themes

The seven examples differ in content, but the decision structure stays compact. Something appears. The mind feels pressure to settle it. A repeated internal action begins. That action has a stopping rule, often certainty, relief, completeness, or a particular feeling. Response prevention removes the certainty procedure while ordinary responsibilities remain.

When a new theme arrives, resist the temptation to build a new philosophy for it. Start with function. What is the question asking you to do? Which internal action are you repeating? What would count as enough if OCD were setting the standard? What is the ordinary standard instead? Where is the Answering Line?

You do not need a perfect classification before practicing. Catch one repeated response and reduce it. The theme can stay complicated while the behavioral choice becomes simpler.

Appendix H: A Thirty-Day Practice Plan

This plan is not a treatment prescription and it does not replace individualized care. It is a way to organize the skills in this book so that practice does not become another endless project. If you are working with an OCD clinician, use that treatment plan instead when it differs from this one.

The central rule for all thirty days is simple: measure practice by behavior, not by whether you feel certain, calm, convinced, or finished.

Days 1 to 5: Map before changing

For the first five days, make discrimination the main task. Choose one or two recurring episodes per day and record them after the episode is over. Identify the trigger, the first obsessional signal you noticed, the mental or behavioral response that followed, and the point at which the response became repetitive.

Do not attempt to catalog every thought. A complete inventory can become checking. The goal is to make one loop visible.

On Day 1, notice one episode of mental review. On Day 2, notice one episode of internal reassurance. On Day 3, look for a feeling check. On Day 4, look for a neutralizing strategy that sounds helpful or reasonable. On Day 5, choose the pattern that costs the most time or freedom and make it the first target.

At the end of this phase, write one sentence that begins: "When I feel pressure to know whether _____, I tend to _____." The second blank should contain an action, not an emotion. "I tend to replay the conversation" is more useful than "I tend to get anxious."

Days 6 to 10: Draw the Answering Line

During the next five days, practice locating the boundary between what arrives and what you recruit to answer it.

On Day 6, mark the first deliberate mental move after an obsession. On Day 7, identify the stopping rule. Are you trying to reach certainty, relief, a right feeling, a complete memory, or moral innocence? On Day 8, notice the fastest micro-ritual, such as one sentence of reassurance or a quick internal comparison. On Day 9, notice a substitute ritual that appears when you block the obvious one. On Day 10, write a one-line response-prevention target.

A useful target sounds like, "When that doubt appears, I will not replay the conversation to decide what it meant." A vague target such as "I will stop overthinking" is harder to practice because it does not say which action to prevent.

If you only notice the line after the ritual has been running for ten minutes, count that as data. The next opportunity begins with the next loop, not with punishing yourself for the one you missed.

Days 11 to 15: Practice non-engagement

For five days, use the three moves from Chapter 9: notice, decline, return.

Keep the decline brief. You do not need a perfectly worded response. "Not solving that now" can work if it is used as a cue for behavior rather than repeated until it produces relief. You can also skip words entirely and move directly to the return.

On Day 11, practice with a mild recurring doubt. On Day 12, practice after a memory urge. On Day 13, practice when the urge is to check a feeling. On Day 14, practice when reassurance is available from another person or a device. On Day 15, practice in a normal activity that matters to you.

The return should be concrete: finish the email, wash the dish, keep walking, listen to the next sentence, turn the page. Returning to life is not a trick for erasing the obsession. The thought is allowed to remain while behavior moves elsewhere.

If non-engagement begins to sound like a debate, shorten it. If "maybe, maybe not" becomes a repeated charm, stop repeating it. If returning becomes frantic distraction, slow the action and let the thought remain present.

Days 16 to 20: Add response prevention to planned exposure

Now choose a modest exposure that targets the unanswered question without creating genuine danger. If you are new to ERP, have severe symptoms, are uncertain about the formulation, or the theme involves significant medical, legal, trauma-related, or safety concerns, planning with a qualified professional is the safer route.

On Day 16, define one feared question and one ritual you will prevent. On Day 17, practice the exposure once without grading your anxiety. On Day 18, repeat it in a different context. On Day 19, reduce one substitute ritual that appeared afterward. On Day 20, review what you learned about your behavior.

Keep exposures connected to real life when possible. Leave a normal message without rereading it five times. Finish a routine task without checking how complete it feels. Let a remembered conversation remain partially uncertain. Read a short uncertainty statement and then resume the day.

Do not turn the exposure into a punishment. More distress is not automatically more useful. The target is learning with response prevention, not proving toughness.

Days 21 to 25: Generalize into ordinary life

During these five days, move away from special practice periods and toward natural moments.

On Day 21, use the method during work or study. On Day 22, use it in a relationship without asking for one extra confirmation. On Day 23, use it around online searching by setting an ordinary information limit. On Day 24, use it during an unstructured period when rumination usually expands. On Day 25, let one imperfectly completed internal task remain unfinished.

Notice what changes when the ritual is not available. You may feel anxiety, guilt, incompleteness, irritation, grief, boredom, or nothing dramatic at all. None of those reactions is a grade.

The practical question is whether more of your behavior is being chosen by the situation in front of you rather than by the demand for certainty.

Days 26 to 30: Build flexibility

The final five days are about preventing the method itself from becoming rigid.

On Day 26, practice with a different theme than your usual one if a natural opportunity appears. Do not invent disturbing content merely to complete the assignment. On Day 27, allow an exposure to feel imperfect. On Day 28, skip an unnecessary recovery check. On Day 29, write your relapse card using the format in Chapter 16. On Day 30, choose one practice you will keep and one practice you no longer need to schedule.

Your maintenance plan should be small enough to live with. A weekly behavioral review may be useful. Constant self-monitoring usually is not. The purpose of maintenance is to notice a returning pattern early and resume flexible practice, not to prove that OCD will never become loud again.

At the end of Day 30, answer three practical questions once:

What mental ritual do I recognize faster now?

What ordinary action am I more willing to continue without certainty?

What is my first response when the ritual returns?

Write the answers, then stop. Do not repeat the exercise until the answers feel perfect. The plan ends the same way the book's method works: with enough information to choose a next action and room for uncertainty to remain.

Appendix I: Twenty Discrimination Drills

The quickest way to understand covert compulsions is to practice distinguishing a mental event from the work done in response to it. Each drill below gives a short situation, then identifies the likely Answering Line. These are not diagnostic rulings. In real life, context and function matter. Use the drills to sharpen the question you ask, not to create a new checking system.

Drill 1: The email

Noah sends a routine email and immediately thinks, "That sounded rude." The thought itself is the signal. He then rereads the sent message six times, reconstructs the recipient's likely reaction, and silently lists evidence that he is usually polite.

The likely ritual is the repeated review and reassurance work. An ordinary correction would be different: if Noah notices a concrete error, he can fix it once. The Answering Line is crossed when the task shifts from correcting information to proving that no negative interpretation is possible.

Drill 2: The intrusive image

Keisha has an unwanted violent image while holding a kitchen knife. She did not choose the image. She then begins asking whether the image felt "too vivid," checks whether she had any urge, and reviews her history to prove she would never act on it.

The image belongs on the signal side. The deliberate tests and historical case-building belong on the response side. Response prevention does not require Keisha to enjoy the image or call it meaningless. It asks her not to perform the certainty procedures that follow.

Drill 3: The compliment

Ben receives a compliment from a coworker and later wonders whether he responded arrogantly. He remembers saying thank you. Then he spends twenty minutes replaying his tone and comparing it with how a humble person should sound.

The first recollection may be ordinary. The repeated comparison is different in function. The useful question is not, "Am I allowed to remember the conversation?" It is, "What am I asking this replay to deliver?" If the answer is a final moral verdict, the replay is likely functioning as a ritual.

Drill 4: The medical instruction

Elena has been told by her physician to check a specific symptom once daily for a limited period. She follows the instruction at the planned time. Two hours later anxiety rises and she checks again, not because the symptom changed but because she wants to feel sure the first check was accurate.

The planned medical check is ordinary care. The anxiety-driven repeat may be compulsive. The distinction protects both sides: ERP does not cancel legitimate medical guidance, and medical guidance does not automatically justify unlimited checking.

Drill 5: The prayer

Grace has a normal evening prayer practice that matters to her. During prayer, an offensive thought appears. She restarts the prayer five times until it feels sincere and uncontaminated by the thought.

The meaningful practice is not the problem. The repeated restarting in order to neutralize an unwanted thought is the likely ritual. Response prevention can respect the prayer while removing the extra rule: complete the chosen practice by the ordinary religious standard rather than by an OCD demand for internal purity.

Drill 6: The relationship conversation

Priya and her partner have a disagreement. Later Priya decides there is a practical issue to discuss, writes down two points, and schedules a conversation. Before the conversation she also spends an hour testing whether her annoyance means the relationship is wrong.

The practical preparation has a defined task and stopping point. The feeling test asks for a different product: certainty about the relationship through repeated internal measurement. Two forms of thinking can occur on the same topic and have different functions.

Drill 7: The memory gap

Luis cannot remember whether he locked a door at a house he left months ago. There is no current safety action available and no new evidence. He spends the evening replaying the departure sequence, hoping one version will suddenly feel certain.

The gap is a signal. The reconstruction is the ritual. A useful stopping rule is based on actionability and evidence, not on whether memory confidence reaches one hundred percent.

Drill 8: The exposure review

Maya completes an exposure and then asks, "Did I allow enough uncertainty?" She reviews every minute of the exercise and checks whether her anxiety changed in the right way.

A brief planned treatment note can be useful. The repeated audit for certainty about doing ERP correctly can become recovery checking. The treatment skill is not exempt from functional analysis. If the review is serving reassurance rather than a planned clinical decision, it can sit on the ritual side of the line.

Drill 9: The online search

Daniel reads one reputable source to answer a practical question about a software setting. The answer is clear. He then opens twelve more pages because a thought appears that the first source might have missed an exception relevant to a feared outcome.

Searching is not inherently compulsive. The function and stopping rule matter. Information gathering with a defined question can stop when the question is adequately answered. Search that expands because certainty is still imperfect can become reassurance seeking.

Drill 10: The body scan

Sofia notices a normal bodily sensation after exercise. She then checks the same area every thirty seconds to determine whether the sensation is getting stronger, weaker, stranger, or more significant.

The initial sensation is not a ritual. The repeated scan may be. When appropriate medical boundaries are already clear, response prevention can mean leaving the sensation unmeasured between ordinary checks rather than trying to decide what every fluctuation means.

Drill 11: The apology

Aisha realizes she interrupted someone repeatedly. She apologizes once. Later she considers whether a second apology is needed because the first might have sounded insincere. No new interaction has occurred.

Repair and reassurance can look alike from the outside. The first apology addresses a concrete behavior. The second urge may be asking for relief from moral uncertainty. The Answering Line is located by function: is there a new repair to make, or is the mind demanding proof that the repair was perfect?

Drill 12: The "maybe" phrase

Marcus has learned to respond to intrusive doubts with "maybe, maybe not." At first the phrase helps him stop debating. Soon he repeats it eight times until he feels less anxious.

The same sentence has changed jobs. Used once as a cue to disengage, it can support response prevention. Repeated until relief arrives, it can function as neutralizing. The words do not determine whether something is a ritual. The behavior around the words does.

Drill 13: The values statement

Noah reminds himself that he wants to be a caring parent before choosing to put his phone away and play with his child. Later, when an intrusive harm thought appears, he repeats "I am a caring parent" until he feels certain the thought says nothing about him.

The first use helps choose behavior. The second use is evidence offered to settle an obsessional doubt. Values can guide action without being used as a courtroom exhibit about identity.

Drill 14: The ordinary decision

Keisha is choosing between two similar jackets. She compares price, fit, and comfort, then picks one. After paying, she returns to the store twice because she cannot achieve a complete feeling that the choice was correct.

Ordinary decision making often includes uncertainty. The compulsion is not caring about the choice. It is the repeated attempt to remove normal residual doubt after an adequate decision process has ended.

Drill 15: The sleep question

Ben lies in bed and an old embarrassing memory appears. He thinks, “Why did I say that?” He starts reviewing the event because he believes he must understand it before he can sleep.

The memory can remain present without being solved. The ritual is the conditional rule that sleep must wait until the event has been understood well enough. Response prevention can be as plain as leaving the question open and continuing the bedtime routine.

Drill 16: The symptom label

Elena wonders whether a particular thought “counts as OCD.” She looks at her treatment notes once because her clinician asked her to learn a distinction. Ten minutes later she is still comparing the thought with examples and asking whether she is applying the label correctly.

Psychoeducation can be useful. Classification can also become reassurance. When the label is being pursued as a guarantee that the feared content is not real, the diagnostic question itself can enter the loop. A clinician can address genuine diagnostic uncertainty; repeated self-testing is not a substitute for assessment.

Drill 17: The good feeling

Grace finishes a work task and feels satisfied. A second later she checks whether the satisfaction is “too strong,” because she worries that enjoying success means she is selfish. She deliberately recreates the feeling to inspect it.

The original emotion is an experience. The deliberate recreation is a test. The Answering Line is crossed when Grace turns a passing feeling into evidence that must be measured and interpreted.

Drill 18: The family question

Priya asks her sister for the time of a family event because she genuinely does not know it. Later she asks, "You really think everyone is okay with me coming, right?" She repeats versions of the second question after each answer.

Both are questions, but only one is ordinary information seeking. The first has a factual answer that solves a practical problem. The second keeps returning because reassurance has not created durable certainty. Function separates them more reliably than form.

Drill 19: The imagined future

Luis thinks about an upcoming presentation and plans three points he wants to cover. After planning, he spends forty minutes imagining every possible question from the audience and mentally rehearsing answers until he feels protected against embarrassment.

Preparation has a task boundary. Compulsive rehearsal expands the boundary until every possible future must be covered. Response prevention can mean keeping the useful preparation and declining the impossible insurance policy.

Drill 20: The new theme

Maya has spent months working on relationship-related rituals. One day an intrusive moral doubt appears and feels completely different. She concludes that her old tools do not apply because the content is new.

Before building a new strategy, she asks one functional question: "What is my mind trying to make me do for certainty?" She notices replay, self-reassurance, and a feeling check, the same response classes she already knows.

Theme migration can make an old process feel new. The answer is not to assume every new concern is OCD. It is to reapply discrimination: look for the repeated response, preserve ordinary responsibilities, and use the same response-prevention logic when the formulation fits.

How to use the drills without turning them into checking

Read the drills to learn a distinction, then put them down. Do not search them repeatedly for an example that proves your own feared thought is "only OCD." A comparison can teach a skill; repeated comparison can become reassurance.

When you apply a drill to yourself, write one functional sentence at most. Name the trigger, name the repeated response, and choose the next ordinary action. If you are unsure whether a situation reflects OCD, another condition, a real-world problem, or a mixture, bring that uncertainty to a qualified professional rather than using the drills as a diagnostic test.

The skill these examples are designed to strengthen is modest but powerful: noticing when thought has become work. Once that work is visible, response prevention has something specific to prevent.

References

Barkhuff, G. (2026). *Reassurance robots: OCD in the age of generative AI* [Preprint]. arXiv. https://arxiv.org/abs/2602.19401

Craske, M. G., Treanor, M., Conway, C. C., Zbozinek, T., & Vervliet, B. (2014). Maximizing exposure therapy: An inhibitory learning approach. *Behaviour Research and Therapy, 58*, 10-23. https://doi.org/10.1016/j.brat.2014.04.006

Craske, M. G., Treanor, M., Zbozinek, T. D., & Vervliet, B. (2022). Optimizing exposure therapy with an inhibitory retrieval approach and the OptEx Nexus. *Behaviour Research and Therapy, 152*, 104069. https://doi.org/10.1016/j.brat.2022.104069

Gillihan, S. J., Williams, M. T., Malcoun, E., Yadin, E., & Foa, E. B. (2012). Common pitfalls in exposure and response prevention (EX/RP) for OCD. *Journal of Obsessive-Compulsive and Related Disorders, 1*(4), 251-257. https://doi.org/10.1016/j.jocrd.2012.05.002

Hezel, D. M., & Simpson, H. B. (2019). Exposure and response prevention for obsessive-compulsive disorder: A review and new directions. *Indian Journal of Psychiatry, 61*(Suppl 1), S85-S92. https://doi.org/10.4103/psychiatry.IndianJPsychiatry_516_18

International OCD Foundation. (n.d.-a). *Exposure and response prevention (ERP).* https://iocdf.org/about-ocd/treatment/erp/

International OCD Foundation. (n.d.-b). *OCD treatment guide: Best evidence-based therapies, medications, and new options.* https://iocdf.org/about-ocd/ocd-treatment-guide/

International OCD Foundation. (2023, February 2). *Ruminating on ruminations: Mental compulsions and what to do about them.* https://iocdf.org/blog/2023/02/02/ruminating-on-ruminations-mental-compulsions-and-what-to-do-about-them/

Lebowitz, E. R., Panza, K. E., Su, J., & Bloch, M. H. (2012). Family accommodation in obsessive-compulsive disorder. *Expert Review of Neurotherapeutics, 12*(2), 229-238. https://doi.org/10.1586/ern.11.200

National Institute of Mental Health. (2023). *Obsessive-compulsive disorder: When unwanted thoughts or repetitive behaviors take over.* U.S. Department of Health and Human Services, National Institutes of Health. https://www.nimh.nih.gov/health/publications/obsessive-compulsive-disorder-when-unwanted-thoughts-or-repetitive-behaviors-take-over

Parrish, C. L., & Radomsky, A. S. (2010). Why do people seek reassurance and check repeatedly? An investigation of factors involved in compulsive behavior in OCD and depression. *Journal of Anxiety Disorders, 24*(2), 211-222. https://doi.org/10.1016/j.janxdis.2009.10.010

Radomsky, A. S., Neal, R. L., Parrish, C. L., Lavoie, S. L., & Schell, S. E. (2021). The Covert and Overt Reassurance Seeking Inventory (CORSI): Development, validation and psychometric analyses. *Behavioural and Cognitive Psychotherapy, 49*(1), 3-20. https://doi.org/10.1017/S1352465820000703

Sibrava, N. J., Boisseau, C. L., Eisen, J. L., Mancebo, M. C., & Rasmussen, S. A. (2016). An empirical investigation of incompleteness in a large clinical sample of obsessive compulsive disorder. *Journal of Anxiety Disorders, 42*, 45-51. https://doi.org/10.1016/j.janxdis.2016.05.005

Thompson-Hollands, J., Abramovitch, A., Tompson, M. C., & Barlow, D. H. (2015). A randomized clinical trial of a brief family intervention to reduce accommodation in obsessive-compulsive disorder: A preliminary study. *Behavior Therapy, 46*(2), 218-229. https://doi.org/10.1016/j.beth.2014.11.001

Tolin, D. F., Abramowitz, J. S., Brigidi, B. D., Amir, N., Street, G. P., & Foa, E. B. (2001). Memory and memory confidence in obsessive-compulsive disorder. *Behaviour Research and Therapy, 39*(8), 913-927. https://doi.org/10.1016/S0005-7967(00)00064-4

van den Hout, M., & Kindt, M. (2003). Repeated checking causes memory distrust. *Behaviour Research and Therapy, 41*(3), 301-316. https://doi.org/10.1016/S0005-7967(02)00012-8

Wegner, D. M., Schneider, D. J., Carter, S. R., III, & White, T. L. (1987). Paradoxical effects of thought suppression. *Journal of Personality and Social Psychology, 53*(1), 5-13. https://doi.org/10.1037/0022-3514.53.1.5

About the Author

Helena Mae Prescott writes research-led nonfiction about anxiety, attention, and behavior. Her work translates established psychological ideas into clear, usable language while keeping a firm boundary between education and individualized care.

She favors practical distinctions, ordinary examples, and methods readers can discuss with qualified professionals or use to better understand their own treatment.